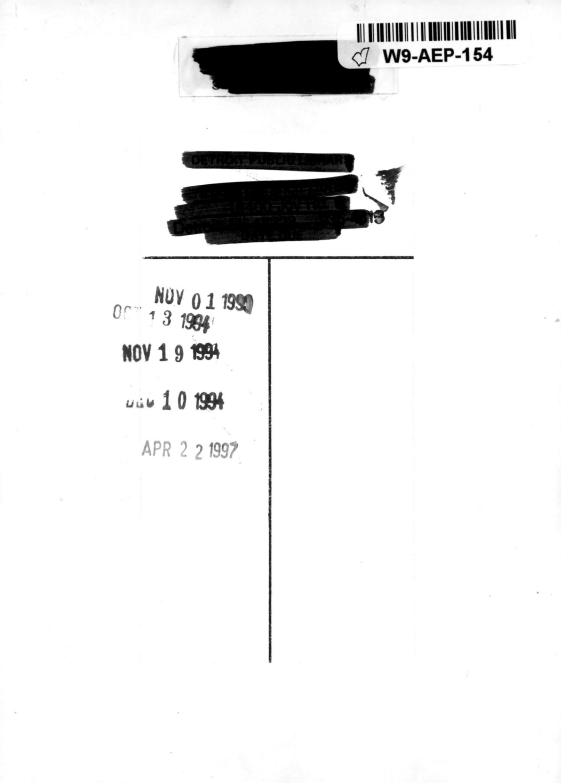

PACIFIC COAST INDIANS OF NORTH AMERICA

PACIFIC COAST INDIANS

OF
NORTH AMERICA

by GRANT LYONS

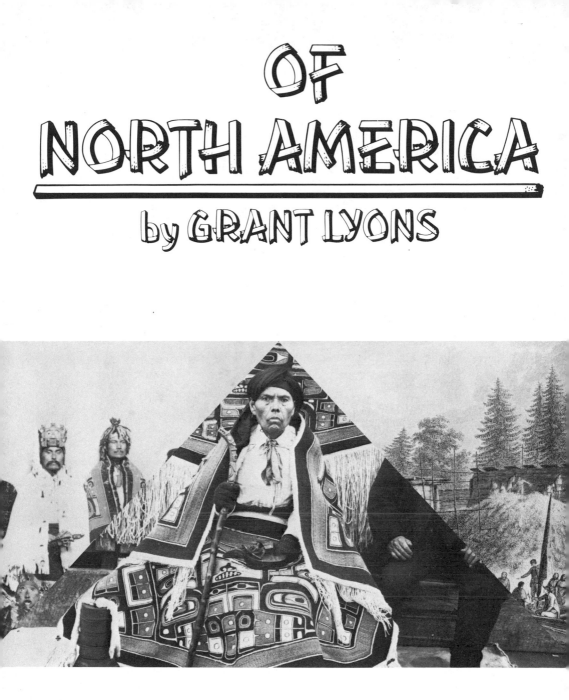

Julian Messner New York

Copyright © 1983 by Grant Lyons

All rights reserved including the right of
reproduction in whole or in part in any form.
Published by Julian Messner, a
Division of Simon & Schuster, Inc.
Simon & Schuster Building,
1230 Avenue of the Americas,
New York, New York 10020

JULIAN MESSNER and colophon are trademarks of
Simon & Schuster, Inc.

Manufactured in the United States of America

10 9 8 7 6 5 4 3 2

Library of Congress Cataloging in Publication Data

Lyons, Grant.
    Pacific coast Indians of North America.

    Includes index.
    Summary: Discusses the culture and history of the
Tlingit, Tsimshian, Kwakiutl, Salish, and other Indian
peoples inhabiting the Pacific coast from Alaska to
California.
    1. Indians of North America—Northwest Coast of
North America—Juvenile literature. [1. Indians of
North America—Northwest coast of North America.
2. Northwest coast of North America—History] I. Title.
E78.N78L97   1983   979.5′00497   82-42877
ISBN 0-671-45801-9

To Sylvia and Irving Kaplan

Messner Books by Grant Lyons

Pacific Coast Indians of North America

The Creek Indians

Mustangs, Six-Shooters, and Barbed Wire

Picture Credits

Alaska Historical Library, pp. 18, 19, 33 top & bottom, 36
    bottom, 42, 43, 66, 111, 115.
British Columbia Provincial Museum, pp. 17, 20, 24, 25, 29,
    31, 40, 67, 76, 104.
Museum of the American Indian, pp. 22, 27, 32, 36, 49, 79,
    53 top & bottom, 105.
Smithsonian Institution, pp. 14, 37, 46, 49, 50, 52, 87.

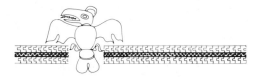

CONTENTS

Chapter 1 / How Raven Made The World   9

2 / The People Of The Far Shores   15

3 / Salmon And Cedar Rich   23

4 / Wealth, Slaves, And Potlatches   34

5 / Guardian Spirits And
    Cannibal Dancers   41

6 / The White Seabird   55

7 / The Great Captain Cook   61

8 / World Crisis At Friendly Cove   70

9 / The Struggle For Alaska   77

10 / The Overlanders   83

11 / The Cold Sick   91

12 / The Oregoners   96

13 / Totem Poles, "Hootch," And Guns   101

14 / Sawmills, Canneries, And Gold   109

15 / Revival   117

Index   125

HOW RAVEN MADE THE WORLD

The Indians who lived along the Pacific coast of North America have a story about how the world was made, and how it came to be the way it is. The old people told this story to their children, who grew up and told it to their children, and so it passed down through the generations and is still told today. This is what they say:

Before there were human beings on the earth, other more powerful beings lived here. They were the First People. They knew many things human beings will never know, they had powers human beings will never have, and they never died. But Raven, the great trickster, changed everything.

Everyone knows the raven is a lazy, wicked—and clever—bird. The Raven Spirit that rules the world is just the same. And he made the world to suit himself.

In those days of the First People the world was completely dark. There was no sun, no moon, no stars, no green trees. Raven himself had no color. Then Raven heard that one family had all the light in the world, but they kept it for themselves. Raven was a thieving rascal then as now, and he decided to steal the light for himself.

The family with all the light had a young daughter who was just reaching the age of marriage. Her family watched over her very carefully to make certain she spoke to no strangers. Raven knew he had to find a way to become a part of this household. The best way, he decided, was to become the baby of the young girl. But how was he to get inside her body and make them think he was her baby?

He made himself into a leaf of a cedar tree and dropped into the family's basket of drinking water. But the girl's mother saw the leaf and threw it out. So Raven made himself even smaller, into the tiny needle of the hemlock tree. This time no one noticed him. The girl drank the water and swallowed the hemlock needle in it.

Once he was inside the girl's body Raven immediately made himself into a baby and began to grow. Neither the girl nor her parents understood what was happening. Very soon Raven was born, a perfect baby, and the family accepted him.

Raven began to cry all the time. He drove the family crazy with his strange wild screams. What is the matter? What does he want? they asked each other. Raven rolled his tricky little black eyes and pointed to a bundle hanging on the wall. They gave him the bundle to play with and he was very quiet for a while.

But when no one was looking Raven tore open the bundle. It was full of the light of the stars. As soon as it was open, the stars scattered, flying up through the smoke-hole of the lodge into the sky.

This was the first light in the world.

Raven began to cry again. He pointed to another bundle on the wall, and again, to quiet him, the family gave Raven the bundle. Inside he found the round, silvery moon. He played with this until the family stopped paying attention to him. Then he threw the moon up through the smoke-hole and into the sky with the stars.

This was the second light in the world.

Raven began crying again. This time he pointed to a handsomely carved cedar box in the corner of the lodge. The family, unable to bear his screaming, gave this to him too. Raven peeked inside and saw that this was the most powerful light by far. It was the sun.

As soon as no one was watching him, Raven

turned himself back into a bird, and with a loud, laughing "Ca-aw!" snapped up the box and flew out through the smoke-hole with it.

He flew to the lodge of his cousin, the seabird, Petrel. There he would be safe. But Raven could not control his desire to steal and play tricks. Petrel owned all the water in the world, and Raven decided to steal this too. So when Petrel was sleeping, Raven took the water into his beak, grabbed the sun-box in his claws, and started to fly away. But Raven's heavy burdens slowed him down.

Meanwhile, Petrel woke up and called on the spirits of his smoke-hole to help him catch Raven. The spirits seized Raven and held him in the smoke-hole while Petrel piled his fire high with pine and spruce pitch. As Raven fought with the spirits, the smoke changed him from snowy white to pitch black.

Finally Raven escaped and flew away. But he found it difficult to fly with the water in his beak, so he began to spit it out. First he spat out the lakes, then the rivers, and finally the sea. And when he saw what he had done, he laughed.

All the First People were now angry with Raven. They came out of their lodges and began shouting at him, saying terrible things about him. This made Raven very angry. He warned them to stop or he would make them sorry, but they paid no attention to him.

Raven opened the cedar sun-box just a little. Some of the sunlight slopped out. It knocked the First People flat on their backs. But still they would not stop shouting and cursing at him. So Raven opened the box all the way.

Sunlight flooded the world. The First People were blasted every which way—some up into the heavens, some into the sea, and some down below the earth.

Raven laughed a long time at what he had done. He thought it was a great joke.

One day Raven decided the world was too empty, so he made human beings. He considered carving human beings from stone so they would last a long time. But he saw that this would take a lot of work. He was too lazy. So he carved them out of twigs and sticks instead. And that is why human beings must die in their season like the leaves of trees, instead of living forever.

Once he had made human beings, Raven saw that they were weak and helpless. So he went to the First People up in the heavens, in the sea, and beneath the earth. He made a deal with them. If they would help the poor weak people he had made, then his people would honor and respect them always. So the First People agreed to return to the earth as the animals and plants human beings need to live—the salmon, the whale, the elk, the deer, the fir and spruce and salmonberry, and many others.

That is why the world is the way it is. Raven made it and it is his world, full of tricks and lies and many jokes on the poor human beings who live in it. Nothing is quite what it seems, and people must die. But friendly spirits are everywhere, ready to help those who honor and respect them.

The Raven—this a mask with moveable beak.

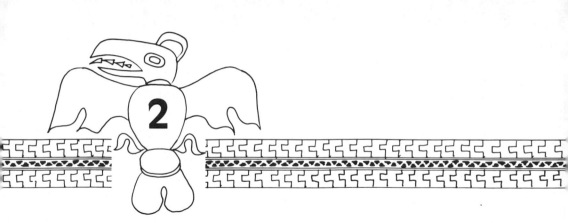

THE PEOPLE OF THE FAR SHORES

The Pacific coast of North America is one of the most rugged and beautiful in the world. There are high cliffs, rocky headlands, thousands of islands, but few beaches. While it is seldom very hot or very cold, even far north in Alaska, savage storms out of the west often beat on the shores for days at a time. Sometimes heavy blankets of fog cover the coast for hundreds of miles, making it impossible to see more than a few feet. And it rains and rains.

The people who lived along this rugged coast, in this mild but unpredictable climate, had no single name, because they did not belong to any one tribe. Indeed, these Indians did not belong to tribes at all.

15

Each Indian identified with his village, and perhaps with one or two other villages nearby, but not with any larger group. Nor did these Indians speak a single language or group of languages. In fact they spoke hundreds of different languages: more languages than all the nations of Europe, and these languages were more different from each other than the languages of Europe.

Despite the different languages, and the fact that the Indians did not identify with nations or tribes, the way of life of Indians all along the Pacific coast was remarkably similar, from northern California to Alaska. It was a way of life built upon the extraordinary abundance of nature on the coast.

Because of the wet climate, plant life along the coast was very rich. California had the largest trees in the world, the redwoods, several hundred feet in height. Farther north, the fir, cedar, hemlock, and pine grew almost as tall. Within these forests the elk and deer were plentiful.

The sea was teeming with salmon and herring, seal and whale and sea otter. In a few months of fishing and hunting the Indian of the coast could obtain enough food to last the entire year.

The Indians' way of life all along the Pacific coast was similar because their surroundings were similar. But another reason was that there was much travel up and down the coast, and useful ideas spread quickly.

To the far north, in the most rugged country of all, where glaciers reach the sea and break off into icebergs, lived three large groups of Indians. On the mainland, and on some of the islands of the Alaskan panhandle, lived the Tlingit (*Tling*-git). On the nearby Queen Charlotte Islands lived the Haida (*Hy*-da). South on the coast and offshore islands lived the Tsimshian (*Tsim*-shee-an).

A Tsimshian village, Gitlakdamix, photographed in 1903.

The Tlingit, Haida, and Tsimshian were more united as peoples than Indians living farther south. Men and women from different villages often married each other and this brought the villages together for feasts and celebrations. Large family groupings formed, called *clans*. These clans identified with some animal or supernatural spirit and included people living in many villages. As a result, the villages sometimes worked together, cooperating with fellow clan-members. All they needed was a common goal or a common enemy. These Indians

Tlingit village at Sitka welcoming visiting neighbors.

A Tlingit leader wearing the robe and carrying the staff that indicate his importance.

were all master wood carvers and canoe makers.

South of the Tsimshian lived the Kwakiutl (Kwa-kee-*oo*-tel) and the Bella Coola. These were two entirely different peoples, speaking different languages, but their villages were so close together that their lives, customs, and beliefs were almost the same. They were also fine wood carvers, but are probably best known for their spectacular religious dances and plays.

South of the Kwakiutl were many villages of Salish-speaking Indians. The Salish lived around what is now called Puget Sound, at the northwest corner of Washington State and the southeast corner of British Columbia in Canada. The Salish built enormous houses, some large enough to house

Salish village of Quamichan, in a photograph taken about 1866.

an entire village of several hundred people! They raised little white dogs and used them like sheep. The dogs were kept in pens and sheared once each year. Their hair was used like wool for blankets.

Northwest of Puget Sound, on Vancouver Island, lived the Nootka, who were famed as whale hunters. Their close relatives, the Makah, lived just south of them, on the Olympic Peninsula of Washington State. The Makah were also whale hunters.

Many other groups of Indians, speaking many languages, lived to the south, along the coasts of Oregon and California. In general these more

southern villages were smaller, and the Indians' lives were simpler than those of the more northern groups. The houses were smaller too and not so well built, the carving of wood was not so expert, and the religious ceremonies less elaborate. But these Indians made excellent baskets out of cedar root and other materials. And some, like the Chinook (Shi-*nook*) of the Columbia River basin, were wide-ranging traders.

The way these coastal Indians lived was designed to exploit the abundance of land and sea. In this they were very successful—so successful that the Pacific coast north of Mexico was possibly the most densely populated area of North America before the arrival of Europeans.

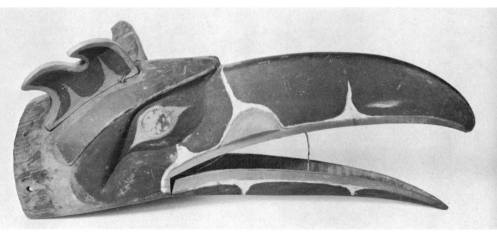

Bella Coola mask—a raven.

SALMON AND CEDAR RICH

Every spring and summer huge numbers of fish moved in from the sea and crowded into the rivers and streams of the Pacific coast. The fish swam upstream to breeding places far inland. There they bred and died. The newly born salmon later swam back down to the ocean to begin the life cycle which would end back where they were born. It was said that you could almost walk across the rivers on the backs of the fish, they were so numerous. The Indians built their entire lives around this abundance of fish.

The most important of the fish was the salmon. The Indians recognized five different kinds, and biologists today classify salmon into the same five groups, or species. The biggest, the Chinook, weigh up to 100 pounds.

All along the coast the Indians knew just when to expect each type of salmon in each stream. They waited. They knew that the fish had to swim very hard against the current. They knew that when the salmon came to rapids or waterfalls they had to hurl themselves through the air to get past. Then the Indians along the shore speared the fish in the air with long wooden spears.

The Indians had other, even better methods for catching the fish. One of these was the *weir*. A weir was like a fence built of wicker or wood across a river. The salmon could not swim around it or leap over it, so they crowded together at the bottom, just

Salmon weir, photo taken sometime between 1867 and 1870.

below the surface. It was an easy matter for an Indian to walk along a platform attached to the fence and spear the fish below by the hundreds.

Such an abundance of fish would have done the Indians little good if they had not found a way to preserve the meat. The fish were cooked immediately, right when they were caught, over slow fires tended by the women. The women squeezed the moisture from the fish and turned them, gradually moving them farther from the flame and more into the smoke. Later the fish were hung in the lodge over the campfires and smoked some more. This smoked salmon lasted the entire winter without spoiling.

Villages, and even families within a village, had claims to certain places on the river banks for setting up weirs or spearing fish. These claims were

Salish Indians with salmon caches, places for drying and curing salmon. Photographed on the Fraser River in 1868.

passed from generation to generation. But there were strict rules about how long a weir could be left in place so that Indians upriver could get their chance, too.

As the fish swam further and further upstream they became more and more exhausted. They lost weight and did not taste as good. Thus, although Indians far inland also speared salmon and other fish, the ones on the coast had by far the richest harvest.

Another important fish that swam upstream in the spring or summer was the *oolichan*. This was an extremely oily fish. In fact, it could be stood on one end and lit like a candle, so that the first white men to visit the coast called it "candlefish." The Indians boiled the oil out of the fish and saved it to add taste to their food during the winter.

The Indians of the coast also caught herring, flounder, sturgeon, halibut, smelts, and other ocean fish in the shallow bays along the coast. For these they used large dragging nets, small dip nets, spears, baited hooks made of hemlock knots, and a special tool called the *herring rake*. The herring rake was like a giant comb with razor-sharp tines. When it was moved through the water, the rake caught the fish on the tines, usually several at a time.

Seals, sea lions, and sea otter were also hunted at sea and along the shore, both for meat and fur. A bull sea lion might weigh 1,500 pounds and could feed a whole village for days. The sea otter, on the other hand, was sought chiefly for its fur, which was thick and soft. It was considered very valuable and only the wealthiest and most important Indians could wear it. The Indians did not think it suitable for poor families to wear.

Another animal that was important to the coastal Indians was the whale. Not many of the Indians actually dared to hunt the huge animals, for this was done with harpoons thrown from small boats and was a difficult and extremely dangerous undertaking. It required a thorough knowledge of the ocean far from land and of the habits of the whales. The Nootka of Vancouver Island, and the Makah, Quinault, and Quileute of the Olympic Peninsula prided themselves on their skill as whale hunters. In each village there were only a few men who were considered experts at throwing the harpoons, and these were the most important men in the village.

The other Indians had to content themselves with the occasional dead whale that washed up on the shore. When this happened it was an occasion for rejoicing and celebration—and hard work. The

Makah basket with design showing hunters in a canoe pursuing a whale.

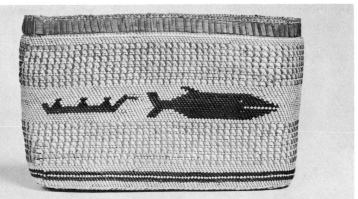

whole village turned out to cut the whale up as quickly as possible so it would not spoil. They boiled the blubber for oil. The oil was stored in a kind of bottle made from a seal stomach. Meanwhile some of the blubber was roasted on the spot for a feast.

Just as important to the Indians of the coast as the swarming fish was the tall cedar tree. The fish provided the chief item of food, but the cedar provided lodging, clothes, transportation, and many of the daily tools.

The cedar is valuable because its wood and bark are water-resistant. For people living in a damp climate, whose lives were spent on the ocean and bays and rivers, this was very important. The grain of the cedar wood is unusually straight and uniform, and this was important for the houses because the Indians built their homes out of boards, not logs. The boards were made by painstakingly splitting a cedar with hammers and wedges.

Most of the coastal Indians had two villages, and so each family had two houses. The summer village was often little more than a camp, so the houses might be simple huts or quickly built shelters. But the winter houses were large and solidly built. The winter houses of the coastal Indians were among the most remarkable achievements of any North American Indians.

The houses built on the coast were generally of two types. Some Indians built their houses of wide boards set perpendicular to the ground and neatly fitted together. Others used narrower boards and strapped them horizontally to a framework with rope, overlapping clapboard style. These overlapping boards could be turned to let in more air or shut tight against the cold.

The houses varied in size among the different groups of Indians but averaged 40 by 60 feet. The Salish-speaking Indians often built much larger houses, 100 feet long or longer. They were often 20

Gwayasdums village photographed in 1900 showing houses made with both horizontal and vertical planks and a handsomely painted house.

feet high or more at the center. To build a house this tall required lifting a huge central rafter to support the roof. In some cases, several rafters were needed. To raise the rafters a ramp of earth was constructed to roll the log up to the needed height.

Just as important to the Indians as their cedar-board houses were the cedar canoes, for the coastal Indian lived on and by the water. His canoes were not made of bent wood and bark like those of the eastern woodland Indians, but were hollowed out of a single cedar log.

Making these canoes was a great art, highly valued by all the Indians. Most villages made their own small canoes for paddling or poling along rivers or across shallow bays. But the larger, oceangoing canoes were the specialty of the Haida, Tlingit, and Nootka, who used them for trading, raiding, and war. They were also traded for by other groups.

The Haida made the largest canoes, 50 to 60 feet long, carrying a dozen or more men. When the first Europeans arrived at the islands of the Haida, they were surprised to find themselves surrounded by canoes almost as large as their sailing ships! Although the Nootka canoes were smaller than the Haida, they were just as well made for ocean travel. They had to be, for use in hunting whales.

The canoe was made by cutting down a suitable cedar tree growing near the bank of a stream so it could be floated down to the village. There it was stripped and patiently hollowed out with a special chopping tool called an *adze*, which was like a hatchet with the blade turned sideways. Once the log was hollowed out it was filled with water and red-hot stones. This softened the wood, allowing the middle of the log to be stretched wide and held with cross-boards, called *thwarts*.

A piece of carved wood was added to the front of the canoe to serve as a spray shield. Carved wood might be added at the back, too. The shield also gave the canoe a graceful, curved shape. Finally, the whole canoe was charred black over a fire to make it more watertight.

The bark that was stripped off the cedar logs was not thrown away because it could be used for clothing. The Indians of the coast wore little clothing, especially in the summer. Most women wore skirts made of shredded cedar bark. The men often wore nothing but a cone-shaped hat to help protect their

Nootka woman weaving a straw hat in 1903. To weave, the straw must be kept soft and pliable by constantly wetting it in the vessel in front of the woman.

eyes from the glare of the sun on the water. The hat was made of cedar or spruce roots twined like straw. Shawls and capes of shredded cedar, worked like coarse cloth, were worn by both men and women in rainy weather. The water-resistant characteristic of cedar made it the most practical material in a climate where leather would soon have rotted away.

The same water-resistance made cedar useful for cooking. Large quantities of food could be cooked in a hollowed cedar log. Food and water were put into the log, then hot stones were added until the food was cooked. Or hot stones were used to cook food in watertight baskets made of tightly twined cedar roots.

When the weather turned cold, the coastal Indian wrapped himself in a blanket. This, too, might be made of shredded cedar. But a woolen blanket was

Cedar bark hat, this belonging to a Haida man, with a painted red and black raven. Women wove the hats, but usually men painted the traditional designs on them.

The blankets covering the Tlingit man on the left are far more beautiful than his companion's jacket.

warmer. The Indians made beautiful woven blankets on hand looms, getting their wool from the mountain goat, or else in trade from the dog-raising Indians of Puget Sound.

Extraordinary example of a fringed blanket of the Chilkat type, used by the Tlingits.

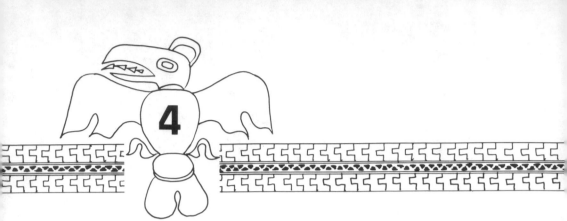

WEALTH, SLAVES, AND POTLATCHES

Compared to other Indians of North America, the Indians of the Pacific coast were rich. Their environment gave them an abundance of everything they needed. They had a surplus of valuable things, and a surplus of time. Indians like the Haida paddled their big canoes all the way down to California to trade. They did not have to go that far to obtain the things they needed to live. They went because they had time to spare, and because they wanted more than they needed, and more, and more.

An awareness of wealth—of one family being richer than another—was rare among the Indians of North America before the arrival of the Europeans. But the Indians of the Pacific coast *were* aware of wealth. It was an important part of their customs, beliefs, and way of life.

In the villages of the coast there was usually no real chief. There was, instead, one man who was richer than the others. Because he was richer, he was respected, and the others followed his lead. Each family knew its approximate position in the ranking. But the leader always had rivals—others who were almost as rich, who were ready to step in and take his place. The rich were the leaders, not only because they were respected, but often because they owned the things necessary for village activities. A raid on another village, for instance, required war canoes and weapons, and the richest families had more of these than the poor. Without the rich, little could be done.

The Indians of the coast were very active traders. What point is there in owning more than you need unless you can use it to trade or to buy things. The Indians also needed money—one kind was a shell, called *dentalium*. This was particularly abundant off Vancouver Island, where it was gathered by the Nootka. It was used by Indians for exchange all along the Pacific coast and by inland tribes as well.

Blankets were also a form of money. The wool for blankets came from mountain goats, which were difficult to hunt. The women spent many long

The long shells are dentalium,
the square shells haliotis.
The design is of a beaver,
and this is a Haida piece.

hours weaving beautiful patterns into the blankets to make them even more highly prized. It was common for the Indians to collect large numbers of blankets just as we save money—either to make a large purchase, such as a canoe or slave, or just to show off. Of course, blankets also kept you warmer than coins!

This Tlingit of many blankets must have been rich.

36

Kwakiutl decorated copper shield, known as "the $100 bill" of the coastal Indians.

Everywhere along the coast the richest families had slaves. A rich coastal Indian who owned many slaves could use them to increase his wealth by having them do various kinds of work, including making canoes, weaving blankets, or spearing salmon. Slaves paddled the rich Indians' war canoes while the owner rode in splendor on a throne.

Although other Indians of North America occasionally made slaves of strangers, only among the

Indians of the Pacific coast was slavery a common part of everyday life. A slave had no rights at all, and could be bought or sold or killed at the pleasure of the owner. Many Indians, like the Haida and the Tlingit, went out regularly on raiding parties to capture more slaves. Usually only women and children were sought on slave raids. The men were considered too dangerous, so they were killed. A male slave child was allowed to grow up, however. He was no threat. By the time he was an adult he knew of no other life than that of his masters, and had no place to escape to anyway.

Most slave raids went from north to south because the Indians of British Columbia and Alaska were richer and more powerful than those to the south. But the Indians of Washington and Oregon sometimes raided each other for slaves. It was not unknown for neighboring villages to raid each other, back and forth, capturing and recapturing slaves.

The richest Indians found various ways of letting others know that they were rich. A flattened head was one sign of having been born into a wealthy family. Among the Indians of Puget Sound and farther south, including the Nootka, rich babies were strapped to a board and another board pressed on their foreheads and strapped down. Gradually the front of the skull was flattened.

Wealthy men often wore robes of fine furs, especially sea otter, as a way of showing how rich they were. Many kinds of self-decoration, such as feathers through the nose, or body paint, were also reserved for the rich. Among the Tlingit, the wealth of a woman could be measured by the size of her *labret*. A labret is a disc, usually of wood, inserted in a slit cut into the lower lip. As the Tlingit woman grew older and got richer, larger and larger discs were inserted. A very rich old woman's lip might flap loosely on her chin. The earliest Europeans did not find this beautiful at all—but the Tlingit did.

The most spectacular display of wealth was the *potlatch*, a Nootka word for party. These parties served several purposes at once. They were a chance for the Indians to enjoy themselves with feasting, singing, and dancing. They were a celebration of important events like marriages and births. They involved much gift-giving so one of the purposes was to redistribute wealth from the richer to the poorer Indians. But the most important purpose of the parties was for the family giving the party to show the others how wealthy they were. The potlatches established the social ranking within the village.

A potlatch was really more than a party; it was a contest. Each family's potlatch was designed to prove that the family was richer than some other

**A family surrounded by their wealth . . .
and enveloped in it.**

family. The more food offered, the more valuable goods given away, the more costly the ceremonies and costumes, the more was the honor to the whole family.

The gift-giving always came at the end of the party. Then the head of each family was called and given a gift. The value of the gift had to be in proportion to the wealth of the man receiving it. The richest men got the most expensive presents, the poorest got the cheapest. If a present was less than the man thought he deserved, he and his whole family were insulted. The only way of wiping out such an insult was for the insulted family to have a potlatch of their own. Their potlatch would then show how rich they were. And the present for the head of the family that had insulted them would be insultingly cheap in turn.

5

GUARDIAN SPIRITS AND CANNIBAL DANCERS

When a boy in an Indian village of the northwest coast reached 12 or 13 years, his life suddenly changed. His father, or another man of his family, took him aside and told him: "Boy, it is time to put away your toys. It is time to become a man. It is time to find your guardian spirit."

For the people of the coast believed that nothing could be accomplished in life without the aid and guidance of a spirit—one of those First People Raven had scattered when he let daylight fill the world. These spirits came back to help the people as salmon, whale, elk, or otter. But they also came back as invisible spirits that entered a human being's soul.

Dance hat, representing a frog. (Tlingit.)

It was a guardian spirit that taught the canoe maker how to make his boats swift, taught the whale hunter where to find the whale, taught the fisherman his skill with a spear. The spirits also taught the right words or prayers to speak, what songs to sing, the secret dances, and the dances to perform for the rest of the villagers.

Unlike some Indians, Indians of the northwest coast did not torture themselves into delirium in order to find their guardian spirits. But each boy did have to face loneliness and conquer fear. The spirits hated fear, and they would give no power to a frightened boy.

When the time came, the boy had to go alone, far from his village, into the deepest woods. This was done in the wintertime, when the people were not hunting or fishing, and when the spirits were willing to come. All day the boy wandered freely through the wilderness. At night he made a fire with his own hands, rubbing sticks together as he had been taught, watching the flames of the fire, the shadows dancing about in the tall trees.

In the morning he bathed in an icy stream or pool, for the spirits came only to the clean. And he wandered, and waited, some more. The spirit might not come for many days and nights of wandering. The boy could not eat anything. If he became too hungry, he returned to his village and told his family that no spirit had come—perhaps next year.

Dance rattles. (Tlingit.)

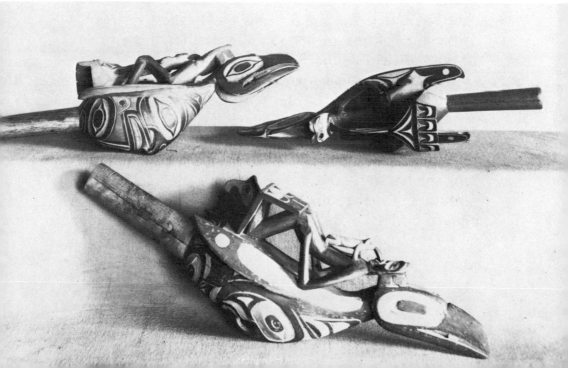

Sometimes, although not often, no spirit *ever* came. Then the future of the boy was doomed. He would never have a skill, never have power or wealth. He would have to do the lowest, most ordinary chores for other people. He would be a failure and his family would be ashamed of him.

Luckily, a spirit usually did come. The boy might be sitting by his fire, trying not to think about his hunger, or about his family and friends who were going about their daily lives without him. But most of all he would try not to be afraid.

Suddenly, an animal would appear—or a bird— or a terrifying monster that was unlike anything on earth. Or branches would break off trees and go flying through the air, and the very earth beneath his feet would begin to shake. The boy would fall back, unconscious, and the spirit would enter into him. It would begin to whisper the first words of the boy's very own magic song, and to show him the first steps of his spirit dance. Thereafter this spirit would always be there to help the boy, to give him strength and courage, and skills.

After his first encounter with his guardian spirit the boy returned to his village and said, "The spirit of the gray wolf has come to me." Or it might be the hare, or the eagle, or the seal. "He has begun teaching me his song and dance. He tells me I will be a hunter." Or the boy might be a fisherman or a canoe builder.

For the men of the coast usually had a specialized skill. The man who built canoes did not have to spear salmon, because he could buy salmon with his canoes. The fisherman sold his salmon for canoes and meat. Most often a spirit instructed a boy to practice the same skill as his father, or some other close relative, maybe an uncle. Then his father or uncle would be able to teach him all he knew. A boy who was to be a fisherman, for instance, would learn how to build a weir, how to make lightning-quick thrusts with the spear, and also the magic words to be said so that the salmon spirits would not be offended. But the boy's skill came from his guardian spirit.

If the boy was not very good at what he did, this showed that he had not been brave when his spirit first visited him. His guardian spirit did not give him strong magic, so the boy was not successful.

In the winter the boy's guardian spirit would return to him when the people sat around their fires in the lodges at night. It was then that the people told stories, danced, and sang. One by one the spirits of all the men would come to them. Each one would feel the spirit enter his heart, and, without willing it, the man would howl and begin to sing his spirit song. And soon he would be up dancing his spirit dance for the others.

When a man leaped up and began his own dance, his relatives would help him. They danced beside

Elegant carved wooden chest used not only for storage and for furniture but as drums as well.

him, imitating his steps—and making sure he didn't dance into the fire in his delirium. The other people beat drums or wooden boxes or canoe paddles with their hands in time to the rhythm of the song and dance.

Sometimes it happened that a boy's spirit did not tell him to follow the way of his father, or even the way of an uncle, but to learn some entirely new skill unknown to his family. In that case the boy had to go to some other family and his father would pay that family to teach his son. This arrangement often led to the two families becoming much closer to each other.

A woman's spirit power was different from a man's. The Indians believed that a woman's spirit power showed itself in her ability to have children—the gift of life itself. The Indians were amazed at this power, and a little afraid of it. In some villages, when a girl reached the age when she could begin to have children—13 or 14—she was shut up for weeks in a dark room without windows. This was because the Indians believed that at this time the girl had so much power that simply by looking at the sun or moon she might knock them out of the sky!

The girls of many villages also had guardian spirits. But these were not so important or so powerful as the spirits that came to the boys. In part this was because the girls could not be allowed to go off by themselves to find their spirits. They might be stolen and enslaved. So a girl's guardian spirit had to come to her as she worked at her daily chores in the village. Such a spirit might help the girl in some skill, too. One girl might be given a knack for finding the delicious salmonberry patches. Another might be given a skill at weaving blankets.

One spirit was more powerful but more rare than the others and came to both women and men. This was the spirit of healing, dream-travel, and spirit seeking. It was a fierce, dangerous, demanding spirit. Those men and women who were seized by this spirit were almost like crazy people, and the others were afraid of them. No one sought such a savage spirit. But when it took hold of you it did not let go.

The healers and spirit callers have been called medicine men and women, or *shamans*. They had the power to fall suddenly into a deep sleep and go traveling in their dreams. They traveled to the spirit villages where they talked to the spirits, who told them many secrets including events to come. But most often the shaman visited the spirits to find the soul of a sick man or woman. The Indians believed that when a man or woman was sick, his or her soul had been stolen by a thieving spirit. If the soul was not brought back the person would die. Only the shaman could bring back a person's soul. Or perhaps the illness was caused by a poisonous object magically put somewhere in a person's body by a hostile spirit. Only a shaman could locate this object and pull it out. But the Indians believed that only a shaman could insert it in the first place! So shamans were not only respected and feared, they were disliked. Whenever any person was injured or became ill, the people believed some shaman somewhere was responsible.

The Indians who lived farthest north on the Pacific coast had the most elaborate spirit dances. Some were almost like theatrical performances. In addition to the individual songs and dances they

Carved bone "soul catchers" used by shamans to recapture souls taken by spirits.

had group songs and dances. The group dances were performed by special dancing societies. Each dancing society had its own way of dancing, its own ceremonies, its own magic tricks to frighten the audience, and its own secrets. These secrets often included stories about the dancers' ancestors or some legendary hero or spirit. During the dances the members wore elaborately carved masks that represented these ancestors or spirits. Often they looked like ferocious demons.

Among the Kwakiutl the most important dancing society was called the Hamatsa, or Cannibal Dancers. Only the luckiest and wealthiest men in a village were invited to join the Hamatsa. The Hamatsa performed their chief ceremonies during

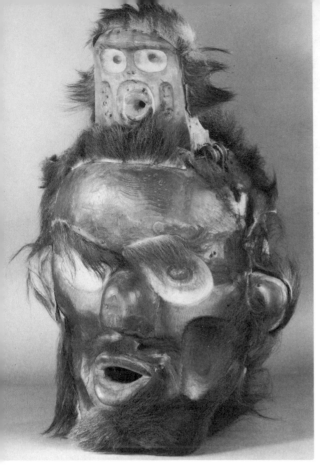

Demon double mask for the winter dances.

the special part of the winter season called *tsitsika*.

Tsitsika means "time when nothing is real." Tsitsika was a time of make-believe, when the Hamatsa would act out events and stories for all the others that *seemed* to be real, but were not. The others in the village might be frightened by some of the things the Hamatsa did, but everyone knew that what he saw was not *really* happening.

Tsitsika was announced at dawn by special eerie-sounding whistles blown by Hamatsa members hidden in the forest around the village. The celebrations were about to begin!

In the middle of the parties, however, the Hamatsa, the Cannibal Dancers, would suddenly appear, acting like madmen, tearing everything up and biting people on the arms as though hungry for human flesh. Right behind the Hamatsa came the Bear-men, another secret society. The Bear-men also acted as though they had gone mad, running about on all fours and growling like bears, barging into people's houses and destroying their property.

The people did not worry about this destruction, however, because right behind the destructive Hamatsa and Bear-men came special society members who carefully noted everything that was destroyed and paid for it all, down to the smallest bone spoon.

The dances were held at night. The Cannibal Dancers climbed up onto the roof of the dance lodges and suddenly dropped down to the floor through spaces were the roof boards had been moved aside. Again they would try to eat the flesh of the others as they danced in a frenzy and acted out the stories of their ancestors, or of the heroes of the secret society.

The masks worn at these dances were often marvelous works of art. Some were very complicated, with moving parts operated by sticks or strings

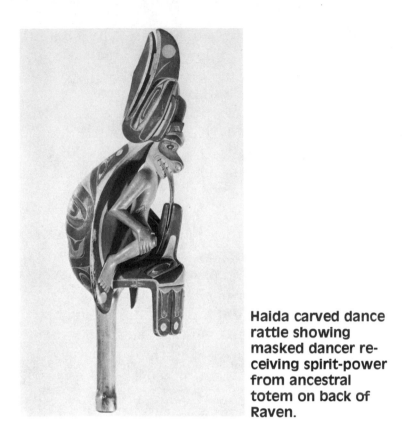

Haida carved dance rattle showing masked dancer receiving spirit-power from ancestral totem on back of Raven.

held by the dancer or his assistants. Some masks were three masks in one, so that the dancer could transform himself from one creature to another before the eyes of his audience. A snake monster would unexpectedly split open to reveal a bear face underneath. Then the bear face would open its mouth wide to show a human mask deep in its throat.

52

**Mechanical mask
with seagull on top.
(Kwakiutl)**

**Same mask, showing how the mask is opened and an
Inner mask displayed.**

Sometimes one of the chief dancers would "die" and disappear completely. This was possible because a secret trapdoor had been prepared beforehand, with an underground passage leading away from the lodge. Later the missing dancer could reappear as though he had come back from death.

Another trick was for one of the dancers to be "beheaded." His head would be lopped off with a knife and would roll on the floor. But the head would turn out to be made of wood carved to look exactly like the dancer's!

The Hamatsa and the Bear-men were only two of the many dancing societies among the Kwakiutl. Each village along the entire coast had its own societies, dances, and "special effects," or tricks. Membership in the societies depended upon being related to other members and upon wealth. Thus the potlatches that established the rank-order in each village, the winter ceremonies and dances, and the relationship of each family to the others, were all fitted together in the coastal Indians' lives.

THE WHITE SEABIRD

For many hundreds of years the people of the Pacific coast lived their lives as their ancestors had. In the summer the salmon swam up the rivers and gave them food in abundance. In the winter the spirits of the First People visited them in the lodges in the flickering firelight. Although they knew all the coast and its peoples from California to Alaska, the Pacific coast Indians knew little or nothing of the Indians who lived inland, beyond the barrier of the mountains that reached to the clouds.

They did not even dream of that other people, who sailed across another ocean, thousands of miles away, to lay claim to the land they called

America. The Indians of the Pacific knew nothing of the squabbles of these white-skinned people—the English, the Spanish, the French, the Dutch—about who owned what part of America. And then, one day, something strange happened . . . .

It was 1579, 87 years after Columbus's first arrival in America. A strange thing, like a giant white seabird, appeared off the coast of what is now northern California. Like certain kinds of gulls, it seemed to fly very low, right at the surface of the water. Gradually it came closer, and as it did so, it looked less like a bird and more like a giant canoe, racing over the surface of the water.

In the canoe were many men with reddish-white skins and hair on their faces. Some of the men climbed tall poles that reached high above the canoe, and white blankets that looked like wings flapped from the poles.

It was an English ship, sailing into waters never before visited by a white person. The captain, a short, thick ruddy-faced man, was no ordinary sailor. He was Francis Drake, the favorite of Queen Elizabeth, and as bold a sailor as ever put his foot on a deck.

Drake knew very well that he was in a part of the world no one had ever seen before. He had come partly by design, partly by accident. One of his many instructions from Queen Elizabeth was to search for a sea passage through North America, later called a Northwest Passage.

Drake had sailed across the Atlantic, down the Atlantic coastline, around the tip of South America, and up the Pacific coast. Coming around the hump of California he had hit terrible weather. His ship had struggled against the winds and currents and had been damaged in the process. Now he was coming in toward land, looking for a safe harbor.

Drake could see nothing on the shore, but eyes were watching him in amazement. Hidden, the Miwok Indians were the first to witness Europeans landing on the Pacific coast of North America. The Miwok lived north of San Francisco Bay, in an area that now includes Point Reyes National Park. In fact, it was toward the southern side of Point Reyes Peninsula that Drake was sailing.

Drake sailed into a sheltered bay—Drake's Bay—and sent men ashore to scout the country. Finding no one, he ordered his crew ashore to haul the ship out of the water for repairs.

Drake was being cautious, and he had good reason to be. He did not know what kind of people he might find in this unexplored part of the world. He was also worried about the Spaniards. He knew they would like nothing better than to capture his ship, the *Golden Hind*, and the man they called, in fear and hatred, "El Draque."

England and Spain were not at war in 1579, but they had been shortly before, and they would be again soon. The actual wars came and went, but the rivalry remained. Each country saw the other as its chief competitor for control of the entire world. Drake was not, at the moment, in her Majesty's Royal Navy. He was sailing as a privateer, although he had the unofficial backing of his queen. So far, Drake's privateering against the Spanish had been very successful.

The Spanish were south of California, and the only Europeans on the Pacific coast of America. They had reached the coast overland, not by ship. They had conquered the kingdoms of the Incas and Aztecs and their ships were busy carrying off loot across the Atlantic to Spain. Drake knew that on the Pacific coast, where Spain had no war ships, he would have an easy time of it. And he did. Raiding up the coast of South America and Mexico, he had captured a treasure in Spanish gold and silver.

He had also captured Spanish maps. From them he saw that the Spanish knew absolutely nothing of the coast north of Mexico, although they had claimed it for Spain. They had drawn only a vague line for the coast, and called it all "California." Drake knew this was a name taken from a book of make-believe. He decided to explore the lands north of Mexico.

A few days after their arrival, the Englishmen had unexpected visitors, a small group of naked men. They carried bows, arrows, and spears, but did not look as though they intended to attack.

The two groups of men met, and in sign language they tried to explain themselves to each other. The

Miwok were curious about these strange people who had arrived in an even stranger canoe. But they were worried, too. This part of the coast belonged to them, and they allowed no one else to dig for clams here. Did the big-canoe people plan to take their clam beach from them?

Drake explained as well as he could that they were only stopping to fix their ship. Then they would sail away again. They did not want the clamming beach. But they certainly would not mind help in finding fresh food!

The Miwok, satisfied that the newcomers meant them no harm, brought them fresh salmon. They also brought cakes made from acorn meal, and a vegetable that looked like an onion but was really the bulb of the beautiful blue camas lily. Gradually they even brought their women and children to see the strangers, men who covered their bodies in cloth, had hair on their faces, and made "gna-ah."

To the Miwok the "gna-ah" was the best thing about the strangers. It was a word they invented for the sound the Englishmen made when they sang hymns. Whenever the Indians came to visit they would first make speeches, long speeches with many gestures, as though they expected the English to figure out what they were saying. Then they would give the English some salmon and politely request some "gna-ah."

The English, in turn, were happy to sing for their supper, so the two groups got along well during the five weeks it took to repair the ship. The Miwok also showed the English how they used weirs to trap salmon, how they netted fish in the bay, and how they boiled their food in watertight baskets using hot stones.

When at last Drake's ship sailed away, the Miwok were sad. As was their custom, the women scratched their faces till the blood ran, to show their grief at the loss of their new friends, while the men climbed to the highest cliff to wave good-bye as long as the ship was in sight.

Drake finally made his way back to England where Queen Elizabeth accepted the Spanish gold he brought her, and in gratitude made him *Sir Francis Drake*. And the faraway land he had discovered was called "New Albion," using the ancient Greek word for England itself.

Drake's voyage brought the first information about the people of the Pacific coast to the rest of the world. But it was a long time before anyone else was able to add anything to what Drake had learned about the Miwok.

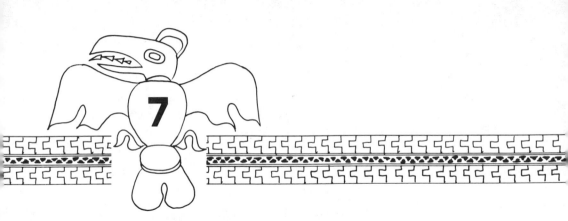

THE GREAT CAPTAIN COOK

Drake's sudden and unexpected raid on the Pacific coast of Spanish America alarmed the Spanish. Time passed, however, and few English ships managed to round the tip of South America, much less sail north all the way to California. The Spanish also found it difficult to explore north of Mexico. The winds and currents along the coast made it all but impossible. Occasionally a Spanish ship sailing *east* across the Pacific from the Philippines came in sight of the northern coast, but these ships did not land.

As a result, the northern coast remained a mystery to Europe for another 200 years after Drake.

When the Spanish did finally get around to establishing a better claim to California and the northern coast, they were responding to a threat from the Russians, not the English. A Dane named Vitus Bering, sailing for the Russian Czar, had discovered the sea route between Siberia and America in 1728. On later voyages, both Bering and a Russian captain crossed the Bering Sea to Alaska. In the 1760s, the Spanish believed the Russians planned to build a fur empire in northwest America.

To make their claims to California stronger, the Spanish sent their first colonists to "Alta California," or Upper California, in 1769. This colony, on San Diego Bay, consisted of soldiers, Catholic priests and monks. Besides colonizing the land for the Spanish, their purpose was to make Christians of the Indians—by persuasion if possible, by force if necessary.

More colonies or missions were established along the California coast in the following years. The pattern was always the same. The Spanish soldiers rounded up the Indians and forced them to live in or near a fortress which the Indians had to build themselves. The Indians had to give up their way of life and work hard for the soldiers and clergymen. They were also forced to give up their beliefs and accept the Catholic religion.

Eventually 21 missions were built in what is now the state of California. However, these missions reached only as far north as San Francisco Bay. So the Miwok and other Indians living further north remained untouched, although Spanish ships did occasionally explore the northern coast for signs of the Russians. They found no signs and they did not land.

In the meantime, the British had not forgotten Drake's "New Albion." They believed Drake's voyage gave them a good claim to the Pacific coast, and eventually they did something about it. In 1778 they sent a great sailor and explorer to explore New Albion and beyond, and to look for that Northwest Passage through the Americas.

The sailor's name was Captain James Cook. Born poor, Cook had worked for years as an apprentice shipbuilder in a London boatyard before signing on with the British navy. He proved so capable that he quickly rose to captain. By the time he sailed to the Pacific coast of North America, Cook was already famous. On two voyages around the world he had discovered New Zealand and New Caledonia, and he was the first to sail into the Antarctic Ocean. On this trip, on his way to America, he had discovered the island of Hawaii.

Cook was an extremely exacting man, and as a result he found many other things besides new lands. Wherever he sailed, he mapped the coastline very carefully and charted winds and ocean currents, making it easier for other explorers who came after him. He devised a method for calculating exactly how far east or west his ship was while at sea. And he learned that eating fruits and vegetables rich in Vitamin C prevented scurvy, a disease that every year killed hundreds of sailors.

Reaching the Pacific coast of America in March, 1778, Cook immediately began his careful mapping of the coast, the winds, and currents. His two ships, the *Discovery* and the *Resolution,* sailed slowly along the coast of the present state of Washington until they ran into typical northwestern weather. Battling storms for weeks, they finally pulled into the shelter of what is now called Nootka Sound on Vancouver Island.

Cook's welcome was somewhat different from Drake's. His ships were no sooner in the sound than they were surrounded by swarms of canoes full of armed Indians.

Some of the canoes were small, for one or two Indians. Others were a full thirty-feet long and full of men waving bows, arrows, and spears, and shouting at the tops of their voices. The Indians paddled their canoes round and round Cook's ships at amazing speed. On some of the bigger canoes the Indians were dancing and singing. On others, Indians in robes of fur appeared to be trying to deliver speeches. Finally one of the biggest canoes approached and an Indian scattered red powder and white feathers on each of Cook's ships in turn. Cook interpreted this as a gesture of peace, and he was indeed correct.

One Indian seemed to be the leader. He did not squat down in his canoe, but rode in a chair, high above the others, while many Indians paddled his big canoe for him. His body and arms were painted red, his face white, and he had feathers tied into his hair so that they stuck out in all directions.

This Indian was Makweena, the most important—and wealthiest—Indian of the Nootka village nearest the British ships. Eventually he came aboard Cook's ship, and in sign language managed to tell Cook that he was not the first European to visit the Nootka. Two years before, a Spanish ship had come into the sound. The Spanish had given the Indians gifts, but refused to come ashore. Now Makweena was inviting Captain Cook and his men to come ashore and be guests of the Nootka.

Perhaps Captain Cook was more adventurous than the Spanish captain. Perhaps, unlike the Spanish ships, Cook's ships had not been attacked by coastal Indians. In any case Cook accepted Makweena's invitation. In the morning he went ashore to visit the village. Wherever he went, Captain Cook made it a habit to carefully observe the people he met in strange lands and to make notes on them. The Nootka were no exception. Cook left an excellent description of the people.

Cook noted that the Indians frequently said "wakah," or "wakas," which seemed to mean "welcome," or "friend." So Cook called their language "Wakash," and that is what Nootka and related languages are called today.

The Indians themselves he described as short and thick-bodied. He noted that the heads of most of them were oddly flattened and that both men and women had misshapen legs. He reasoned that this was due to daily life in a canoe from childhood on. The Indians' bodies were painted, and they were naked except for a few of the most important men, who wore long cloaks of a beautiful soft fur. Some of the men had long thin moustaches and beards, and many wore ornaments thrust through their noses.

This Tlingit head man wears a nose ornament as the Nootka did.

The village consisted of three neat rows of houses, all made solidly of wood, with pointed roofs and clapboard walls. Cook was taken as guest of honor into Makweena's house, and he observed that the floor was below ground level and was covered by reed mats. At the center of the lodge several fires were burning under cooking pots, each surrounded by a safety area of sand brought up from the beach. Several families shared the lodge, and each family had its own area marked off from the others by handsomely carved cedarwood boxes, inside which the Indians kept their household tools.

This scene of the Nootka was drawn by a member of Captain Cook's crew in 1778.

At one end of the lodge the huge posts that held up the rafters and roof had been carved to look like animals or monsters. Cook noted that although the Indians respected these idols, they did not worship them. The walls were also hung with reed mats, and on top of these hung numerous wooden masks which astonished the English by their artistry.

Cook spent several weeks with Makweena. Some days Makweena gave a feast, chiefly of salmon and berries. Other days, Cook feasted Makweena and his relatives. Meanwhile the Englishmen refitted their ships and listened to long speeches they could not understand from the Indians. Everywhere on the coast the Indians loved to deliver speeches!

Finally Cook sailed away to the north, looking for the Northwest Passage. In his usual thorough way he mapped the entire coast all the way to and around Alaska, sailing into the Arctic Ocean. Still he found no Northwest Passage, and he concluded that none existed. Finally, he turned his ship westward and sailed to Hawaii.

In Hawaii the career of this great explorer came to a sudden and unhappy end. In a petty quarrel with native Hawaiians he was unexpectedly attacked and killed, right before the eyes of his crew. His ships sailed on without him, first to China, then to England.

When Cook's ships reached England they brought word of the wealth to be had in New Albion. While sailing along the Pacific coasts, and while living with the Nootka, the men had taken many opportunities to trade with the Indians. One trade item the English especially liked was sea otter fur. Then, when the ship reached China, the Englishmen discovered that the Chinese also loved sea otter fur. The Chinese would pay a great deal of money for even one of these furs. They valued them above all other furs. The crews of the ships were so excited by this discovery that their captains had a difficult time getting them to sail on to England. They all wanted to sail back to America to get more furs and sell them to the Chinese for a huge fortune.

Word of the wealth to be made selling sea otter furs to the Chinese soon spread to Europe and even to the newly independent United States. Adventurous sailor-merchants were not long in following it up. Almost overnight, the people of the Pacific coast, invisible to the rest of the world for so long, found themselves right in the middle of the world stage.

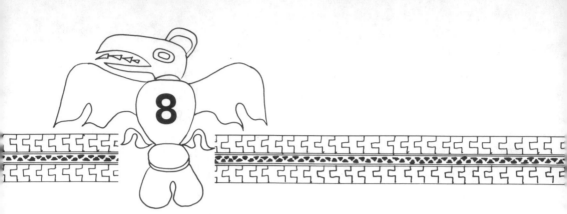

WORLD CRISIS AT FRIENDLY COVE

In the years following Captain Cook's visit, Makweena's village was visited by other white men's ships, and there was a brisk trade in sea otter furs. Besides King George's men, as the British were called, and King Carlos's men, the Spanish, there were also many "Boston men" from the United States.

Makweena and his village tried to be friendly to all visitors. The trade with the white men brought them many wonderful things, including tools made of iron, guns, brightly colored cloth, and blankets. But it was obvious to the Indians that the white men were not necessarily friendly to each other. Then one day in the year 1789, something terrible happened between the white men.

Five of the white men's ships stood at anchor in the sound. They looked very peaceful in the evening light. The largest was a Spanish warship. Makweena knew that it had guns that could make splinters of his biggest canoe with a single loud roar. The other ships belonged to King George's men and the Boston men.

The Boston men had been on the cove since the previous winter. They had come with many presents. They had paid Makweena's village for land to build their lodges on. Then the big Spanish ship had come, and shortly afterwards, the first of King George's ships. At first King Carlos's men and King George's men seemed friendly. But the Spanish captain, Martinez, proved as tricky and deceitful as Raven. One night he had taken the British ship by surprise and put its captain in chains.

When a second British ship arrived, Martinez did the same to the men on it. Did he plan to make slaves of the British? Makweena did not understand everything, but he did know that King George's men and King Carlos's men were arguing about who owned Nootka Sound—and even Makweena's own village. This made him mad. The Nootka did not belong to any king across the sea!

And then, even as Makweena looked out over the sound, he saw something that made him feel even more afraid. For a single small canoe was moving rapidly toward the big Spanish ship. A man, woman, and child were in the canoe, and Makweena recognized them—Kelekum, his own brother, and his young family.

Kelekum was even angrier than Makweena at Martinez. Kelekum had become close friends with the King George's men. He had made them feel so at home that the British called the cove in front of the village "Friendly Cove."

Now Kelekum's canoe turned sharply as it closed on the Spanish ship. Makweena saw Kelekum stand up and heard his voice across the still cove:

"*Martinez pisee! Martinez capsil!*"

Makweena winced at these words—very bad words in the Nootka language. Luckily none of the Spanish knew a word of Nootka. But what if there were some Boston men on board? Some of the Boston men did know Nootka words after their long winter stay.

Kelekum continued shouting at the Spanish ship. A voice came from the ship, shouting something back in the Spanish language, but Kelekum paid no attention. Makweena thought that Kelekum was safe as long as he stayed in his canoe. The Spanish could not grab him, for his canoe was much quicker than any Spanish boat. Still, Makweena was afraid.

It was bad for Kelekum to let himself be drawn into the quarrels of the white men.

Suddenly there was a loud snapping sound. Makweena recognized it—the sound the terrible fire-sticks made. He saw Kelekum fall backward into the water.

Immediately Makweena shouted for help and a canoe sliced across the water toward Kelekum's canoe. After a few minutes it came back with Kelekum's wife and child. But Kelekum was dead in the water.

Many of the men in the village wanted to attack the Spanish ship. The Spanish had no business coming into their place, taking their friends as slaves, and then killing Kelekum. But Makweena restrained them. He was thinking how easily the Spanish had killed Kelekum and how easy it would be, from their big ship, to blast the canoes out of the water and kill many more people. Makweena could see that the Spanish were on the deck of their ship, ready for trouble.

Makweena was the leader of the village; it was his brother who had been killed—and he decided to leave the Spanish alone.

Makweena ordered the village moved to a place where the big ships could not go. When the Spanish ships returned to the cove the following year they found the village abandoned. But the crisis was not over. In fact, it had only just begun.

Europe, so far away, was about to go to war over Makweena's village. King George was not about to allow his ships to be captured and his men put in chains without a fight. And the British had the most powerful navy in the world.

The Spanish captain, Martinez, had been following what he thought were his orders. He had been told to explore the entire coast and to look for foreign ships. If he found any, whether British or Russian, he was to drive them away. He did not worry about the Boston men, because the United States was such a young nation and made no claim to own the Pacific coast.

Now the British demanded the return of the captured men and ships—and also a permanent trading post at Friendly Cove, to make it clear to all that this land did *not* belong to Spain. This was a direct challenge, but at the moment King Carlos was in no position to go to war without the help of her ally, France, and France was busy with a revolution. King Carlos also knew that in any war with Great Britain many of the Spanish colonies all over the world would be lost to the British navy. Spain had to back down and give in to the British demands. The British immediately sent a naval squadron to take over Friendly Cove.

The treaty between Britain and Spain was called the Nootka Treaty. Spain agreed to let all nations trade with the coastal Indians north of the California missions. It was the beginning of the end of the great Spanish empire. At first, few in Europe realized the importance of the Nootka Treaty. Then they realized that the treaty showed that Great Britain, because of her navy, was strong, and Spain, despite all her colonies, was weak. Less than twenty years later the Spanish empire was dead, as her American colonies, one after another, broke free from Spain—with British help.

For the Nootka and other Indians of the Pacific coast the treaty meant that many more ships from many nations came to their villages to trade, chiefly for sea otter furs. Most prominent among them was the young United States. The "triangle trade"—between United States' ports, the Pacific coast, and China—brought profits to American merchants and helped the new country get on her feet economically.

Two Americans who had been on the scene at the time of the crisis at Friendly Cove were Captains John Kendrick and Robert Gray. Even as the Spanish and British squabbled, Kendrick and Gray were carefully mapping the sea otter coast. One of Gray's discoveries was the mouth of an enormous river, the Columbia, which had been overlooked by everyone else. In North America the Columbia is second in size only to the Mississippi, but it was hidden from sight from the ocean by a series of sandbars and often by heavy fog.

Gray's discovery of the Columbia would prove very important in the future. But at the time no one—or almost no one—thought the United States would ever make a claim of her own to the Pacific coast.

Makweena's grave, in a photo taken sometime before 1907.

76

9

THE STRUGGLE FOR ALASKA

The British were not the first to discover the value of the Pacific coast Indians' sea otter furs. Russians had been hunting the animals in America for years before the arrival of Captain Cook. But the Russians were far to the north, on the Aleutian Islands off the coast of Alaska. They had been hunting there since shortly after Bering's 1740 expedition.

The Russians had not been sent by their government. They were independent fur hunters and trappers. None were seamen, but they had manned any kind of boat they could find, many of them drowning in the attempt to cross the Bering Strait.

These men, called *promyshlenniki* (pro-*mish*-len-ee-kee), soon found that they were unable to hunt the quick-swimming animals in their clumsy boats. So they forced the natives of the islands, a people called Aleuts, to hunt for them. The Aleuts had quick, highly maneuverable skin boats called *kayaks*. Large groups of Aleuts in kayaks hunted the sea otter so successfully for the Russians that the surrounding seas were soon all but empty of the animals.

Since the waters around the Aleutians were over-hunted, the Russians wanted to establish a trading post much farther to the south. An official Russian naval expedition was sent to search out a site for a Russian settlement. The expedition was led, not by a Russian, but by an Englishman who had sailed with Captain Cook in 1789, Captain Joseph Billings.

As a result of Billings's exploration, the Russians decided to build a trading post at the present site of Sitka, on an island off the narrow southern strip of Alaska known as the "panhandle." In 1799 Alexander Baranov, a Russian, led a fleet of small boats and kayaks, manned chiefly by Aleuts, down the coast of Alaska to the island that now bears his name, Baranov Island.

Baranov knew that he must move cautiously, for he was moving out of the territory of the Aleuts and into the land of the Tlingit Indians. The Tlingit were enemies of the Aleuts and often raided them for slaves. In two previous contacts with the Tlingit the Russians had found them hostile. About a day out of Sitka the sky turned cloudy, and a strong wind began blowing in from the west. The sea was soon whipped up into a white frenzy, and Baranov decided to find a safe harbor.

It was already night when the Russians and Aleuts paddled into the darkness of a harbor beneath a black sky. They could barely see the beach. The men wearily pulled their boats up onto the sand and paused to catch their breath. Suddenly, horrible shrieks and weird screams split the air, and out of the nearby forest horrible-looking monsters appeared and began running toward them.

The Aleuts were so terrified that they ran the wrong way in their panic—right into the hands of the monsters. The Russians held their ground to fight by the boats. They soon saw that these monsters were in fact Tlingit Indians with carved wooden masks on their faces and a kind of armor

The eyes and jaw move, making this fierce mask seem very frightening.

made of thin wooden sticks sewed together. They did indeed look like supernatural beasts as they screamed wildly and beat the Aleuts with clubs.

Those who could, got back into their boats and beat a hasty retreat, paddling into the storm at sea rather than face the savage attack on land. Many men and boats were lost. The Russians had been given a warning: the Tlingit would not be ruled like the Aleuts!

Baranov and his men managed to ride out the storm and reach Sitka the next day. He landed his men in military fashion, putting out guards and digging entrenchments for protection against possible attack. After a few days Baranov met personally with some of the Tlingit on the island and explained that he did not want to fight, only to trade for furs. The Indians gave him permission to stay, but they were not very friendly. Baranov immediately began building a fortress out of logs and mud.

The new Russian colony was called New Archangel. The Russians stayed in the safety of their fort and had as little to do with the unfriendly Tlingit as possible. Parties of Aleuts hunted the sea otter under the protection of armed Russians.

The new post had little to offer the Tlingit, because the Russians had few goods to trade. Supply ships came to the post so rarely that the Russians were themselves barely able to survive, much less trade.

The Tlingit became less and less friendly. The Russians were particularly alarmed to discover that the Tlingit had guns. The Indians who had attacked them at night had used clubs and spears, but those around New Archangel were far better armed. An explanation was not long in coming. An American merchant ship sailed into the harbor, loaded with guns for sale to the Indians.

Baranov argued with the American captain about the guns, pointing out how dangerous the situation was for his tiny colony. The American captain insisted on selling the guns. He was in business, and guns were what the Indians wanted for their furs. The Tlingit, he said, were not unfriendly at all. They always welcomed his ship.

Baranov continued to complain to other American ship captains, but he could not complain too much, because he soon became dependent upon their ships himself. He had to trade furs to the Americans for supplies his post needed, since Russian supply ships seldom reached him.

On a Sunday afternoon in June, 1802, many of the Russians and Aleuts at New Archangel were away for the day, hunting and fishing. Suddenly, the fort was attacked by more than a thousand Indians! Most were Tlingit, although a few Haida had joined the war party as well. Overwhelming the fort, the Indians drove the defenders from building to building and from room to room until the entire fort was in their hands.

When the word reached Moscow that the Russian colony in Alaska had been destroyed, the Russian Czar was furious. He ordered a warship to move against the Indians. It took two years to organize this attacking force. On the ship was Baranov, who happened to be away from New Archangel at the time of the attack. When the Tlingit saw the big warship, with huge cannons aimed at the fortress they had made their own, they decided to open peace negotiations. Baranov went out to meet them.

The negotiations went on for days. Then one morning the Russians noticed that the fort was surprisingly quiet. More than quiet—it was absolutely silent. The entire place was empty, or rather, empty of all life. The Tlingit had slipped away during the night, but to make sure that no noise gave them away, they had killed and left behind the bodies of their small children and dogs.

The Russians built another, larger fort at another location on Baranov Island. But the Tlingit had learned about forts, and so they built one of their own. They located it on a high rock looking out to sea where they could see ships coming from a long way away but could not be seen themselves.

A few years later the Russians started another colony in Tlingit territory on Yakutat Bay. The Tlingit destroyed it completely, and the Russians abandoned the idea.

An uneasy peace followed. The Tlingit did not attempt to attack the big fort on Baranov Island, but every hunting party that left the fort went well armed. The Russians hunted but never ruled in the land of the Tlingit.

THE
OVERLANDERS

In the years following the Nootka crisis the ships of many European nations and of the United States swarmed up and down the Pacific coast. Not all the ships were merchants after furs, however. Both Great Britain and Spain sent well-armed naval ships to explore the coast and to strengthen their claims there.

Commander George Vancouver thoroughly mapped most of the coast north and south of Nootka for Britain. Vancouver had sailed with Captain Cook in 1776. Now he showed that the land of the Nootka was an island by sailing around it, and in honor of his discovery the island was named after him.

Another member of Cook's crew had been an American named John Ledyard. Although Ledyard never managed to get back to the Northwest coast, as did the two others who sailed with Cook, Vancouver and Billings, he proved to be important in drawing official American interest to the area. Ledyard did this not by exploring or mapping but by writing and talking. He wrote a book about his experiences. The book was especially popular in his own country and was one of the causes of the very profitable triangle trade.

In his book, Ledyard stressed the profits that could be made from the furs. Naturally, he wanted some of these profits himself, so he tried to start a fur company of his own. But to do this he needed to borrow money for ships, equipment, and men. No one in the United States would lend him the money, so he went to Europe. His search took him to Paris where he spent many long evenings talking to the young American ambassador to France. Ledyard recounted stories of the Pacific coast, stressing how important it was for the United States to extend her claims all the way to the Pacific. The ambassador was a sympathetic listener. He even encouraged Ledyard in his wildest idea—to cross North America by land.

When Ledyard heard about Billings's expedition for the Russians, he hurried across Europe and the entire continent of Asia to try to join up with it. Billings was willing to take his old shipmate along, but the Russian authorities were not. They arrested Ledyard and deported him.

He died a few years later on an expedition to Africa.

But the American ambassador in Paris had taken his stories and ideas very much to heart. His name was Thomas Jefferson.

In 1801 Jefferson became President of the United States. One of his first projects was to attempt to get more land in North America for his young nation. In 1803 he bought the huge middle third of the continent, the Louisiana Territory, from France. Even before the purchase was made, Jefferson was already planning an expedition to cross North America overland, not as Ledyard had dreamed, from Pacific to Atlantic, but the other way around.

The Lewis and Clark Expedition set out from the Missouri River in 1803. Officially, it was to explore the new Louisiana Territory. But a second purpose of the trip was to reach the Pacific Ocean, specifically the Columbia River mouth. Jefferson envisioned a great nation stretching from sea to sea.

It took two years, but in the autumn of 1805 Lewis and Clark and their weary party at last reached the Pacific. And there, at the mouth of the Columbia, they were welcomed by Indians who were already familiar with Americans and even knew many words in English—especially cursewords!

The Indians all along the lower Columbia spoke Chinook. On the south shore of the Columbia River where Lewis and Clark chose to make their camp, these Indians were called the Clatsop. So the American camp was called Fort Clatsop.

The Chinook were a very energetic and enterprising people, the great traders of the lower Pacific coast. In part this was because of their unique situation on the Columbia River. The Columbia is wide and deep, and the Chinook could canoe many miles into the interior to trade with Indians who lived far from the coast. The trade network reached from the lower Columbia deep into the mountains and plateaus of the American Far West. The Chinook brought their salmon, oolichan, whale oil, and other coastal products up the river to trade for products of the mountain and plateau Indians. Then they got in their oceangoing canoes and brought these goods up the coast to trade with the Indians there.

Like other coastal Indians, the Chinook lived in wood-plank houses, smaller and simpler than those farther north, and they spent most of their lives in canoes. Because the tall red cedar wasn't common in their territory, they made small canoes and bought the oceangoing ones from the Nootka, those canoe-making experts. The Chinook depended upon the annual salmon runs for their livelihood. Their huge nets, hundreds of feet wide, were more suitable than weirs for the great Columbia River.

At Fort Clatsop the Americans depended on the trade and even the generosity of the Clatsop Chinook. The Americans, however, had little to trade. Nevertheless the Clatsop remained helpful and friendly. In fact, rival Chinook villages were soon squabbling among themselves for the Americans' friendship.

American ships became so common that the Chinook knew many of the captains. Other ships

Haida-carved representation of early European sea merchants.

were numerous as well, and the Chinook added hundreds of words in various foreign languages to their own. They were in fact, developing a new language. Eventually this language spread all the way up and down the coast, and was used by Indians and Europeans. It came to be called "Chinook jargon" or simply "Chinook," although it was not, of course, the Indians' original language.

Trade was lively along the Pacific coast among the Indians because each group had some special product that was valued by others. The Chinooks' chief items of trade were clamons, long, heavy ponchos made out of thick elk-hide. This was so tough that the poncho served as a kind of armor, much like the wood-slat armor of the Tlingit.

Captain Gray's discovery of the Columbia, and the overland journey by Lewis and Clark, gave the United States a claim to the Pacific coast to match those of Spain, Great Britain, and Russia. The American claim was further strengthened five years later, in 1811, when an American trading post was established near the Lewis and Clark campsite in what is now Oregon.

The new post was built by the Pacific Fur Company, an American company started by a German-born New York merchant named John Jacob Astor. The post was called Astoria. Astor was active in the "triangle trade," and hoped to use Astoria as a gathering point for furs. The new post was soon involved in trade with the Indians. They sent expeditions to trade directly with the Indians of the interior, which made the Chinook unhappy. It was these expeditions that discovered the beautiful valley of the Willamette River, excellent farming country.

Unfortunately for the Astoria project, war broke out between the United States and Great Britain soon after the post was founded. Most of the employees at Astoria were British or French Canadians. And in any case there was no way of defending the post against British attack. So Astor's representatives sold the fort and all its contents to a British Canadian fur company in 1813.

For the American fur traders were not alone in the Great Northwest.

Even before Lewis and Clark made their way down to the mouth of the Columbia, a Canadian had also crossed North America overland. He was Alexander Mackenzie, one of Canada's greatest explorers.

MacKenzie had earlier discovered the river which empties into the Arctic Ocean and now bears his name. He was a partner in the North West Fur Company of Canada, and his voyages were part of his company's movement into the wilderness of the northwest in pursuit of furs, chiefly beaver. The Canadians dominated the world trade in beaver and other inland furs even as the "Boston Men" dominated the sea-coast trade in sea otter and seal skins.

Then, little by little, the fur-trading posts moved farther west. In a few years, their chief rival, the Hudson Bay Company, bought out the North West Company.

Astoria's name was changed to Fort George, after the British king, George III. And although the Hudson Bay Company now dominated the western fur trade, its great fur empire was an inland one that looked to the east, not the west.

Fort George, however, remained important to the Chinook and other Indians on the coast of what is now Oregon. This part of the Pacific coast became the major center for trade, and the Chinook Indians were important in it. But with the trade of the white men came other things that eventually destroyed coastal Indian life.

11

THE COLD SICK

The white men used brightly painted sticks to mark the safe channels for their ships to navigate the Columbia River. One day a Chinook Indian, thinking the sticks might have some of the white men's spirit-power, pulled one up and put it into his canoe. It was a beautiful summer day in 1829.

By the time the man reached shore he was sweating and shivering at the same time, and he was so weak he could not stand up without help. Others from his village rushed to him and helped him to a campfire where they covered him with blankets. Despite the fire and the blankets he kept shaking violently with cold—and sweating at the same time. The spirit caller was sent for.

But the spirit caller had never seen a sickness like this one before. He could not find any poisoned objects in the man's body. The spirit caller lay down and went into a trance so his soul could visit one spirit village after another to try to find out what had happened to the sick man's soul. But he could not.

The spirit caller decided that perhaps it was the white man's stick pulled from the river that was at fault. So the white man's stick was beaten with clubs, dragged through the dirt, drowned in water, and finally burned up. But the sick man did not get better. Within a few hours he was dead.

Soon, others in the village showed the same signs of illness—the fever, the shivering, the weakness. One by one they died, too.

The "cold sick," as the Indians called it, spread from village to village. It was swift and deadly. Sometimes whole villages became sick almost at once. Within a few hours hardly anyone in the village was left alive. There was no one even to bury the dead. Those who survived fled their villages and never returned. Some died in the wilderness, others were captured and sold as slaves by enemy villages. A few were accepted into villages that were more friendly.

The epidemic of the "cold sick" was probably influenza. It was only one of many diseases brought by the white people to the Indians of the Pacific coast, diseases like tuberculosis, smallpox, and measles. Measles rarely killed white people. Over many years they had achieved some immunity, but the Indians had not. These diseases frightened and angered the Indians. It seemed like white men's magic, an evil spirit-force. The Indians did not know how to fight such strong magic.

The diseases brought by the white men were more dangerous to the Indians than guns. There was often fighting between merchant crews and Indians, but in these battles only a few were killed on either side. Diseases killed hundreds, and then thousands within a few weeks or months.

Everywhere on the Pacific coast epidemics swept through village after village, year after year. One by one entire villages were completely wiped out. Eventually whole peoples disappeared.

Once 20,000 Chinook-speaking Indians lived along the Columbia River and tributaries. By 1840 there were only 2,000. The Clatsop people, hosts to Lewis and Clark, disappeared entirely. Farther up the coast, where 10,000 Haida had once lived on the Queen Charlotte Islands, epidemics gradually reduced the number to 1,000. The coastal Indians were hit particularly hard by disease. They lived closer together than other North American Indians and traded more actively with white men and other Indians. Contact was greater and diseases spread more rapidly from family to family and from village to village.

The Indians' attempts to cure themselves of the new diseases often did more harm than good. The most common treatment for disease among the coast Indians was the sweathouse. The sweathouse was a low hut made of wood and packed earth. It had a narrow door and no windows. The sick person sat inside while hot rocks were pushed in through an opening. From time to time a little water was sprinkled on the rocks. The hut got hotter and hotter. When it was felt that the poisons or evil spirits had been sweated out, the sick person jumped into an icy stream or pond. The sweathouse was similar to a modern sauna, which can be very healthy. But for a person suffering from influenza, smallpox, or measles, it was the worst possible treatment.

Because the Indians believed the diseases were part of white men's magic, they were not always ready to accept help from the white men when they offered it. Among the Tlingit of Alaska, for instance, a Russian Orthodox Bishop, Ivan Venyaminov, tried for years without success to get the Indians to use the recently developed smallpox vaccine. After a particularly terrible year in 1835 the Indians gradually began to accept inoculation, but by then it was all but too late.

In a few decades repeated epidemics reduced the number of Indians living along the Pacific to a fraction of what they had been before. The toll was especially high among the Indians of what is now Oregon and Washington.

Then, in the 1840s, white men began to arrive in greater numbers than before. These men came over land. And they came not to trade, but to stay.

THE OREGONERS

The triangle trade in sea otter furs thrived for a few years and then began to decline. The profits of the European and American sea merchants got smaller and smaller each year.

Several things caused the shrinkage in profits. The Chinese were less willing to pay high prices for furs that were no longer rare in China. But the sea otter itself became more rare because of the intensive hunting by the Indians for sale to the European ships. And as the number of sea otter furs went down, the price demanded by the Indians went up.

The Indians were shrewd traders. They had been trading among themselves for centuries before the white men came. They knew how to drive a hard bargain. They made the white traders compete with each other to get the furs. The Indians also knew that if they did not get the price they wanted, they could keep the furs until the next year when the price might be better. On the other hand, the white merchant, having gone to all the expense of a long voyage, could not afford to leave the coast empty-handed.

As a result there were often bad feelings between Indians and merchants. Some merchants, unable to buy furs cheaply enough to make a profit, attacked the Indians and took the furs by force. The Indians would then take their revenge on the next, often innocent, ship that came by. Such conflicts contributed to the decline in the triangle trade.

On the other hand, the trade in beaver furs and the furs of inland animals increased. This trade did not depend on the coast Indians at all. Even the Hudson Bay trading post at Fort George was a shipping point for furs brought from the interior.

Realizing that the coast was no longer so important, the Hudson Bay Company moved their principal trading post from the coast to a position farther up the Columbia River. The new post was called Fort Vancouver. When Fort George was torn down, the Chinook Indians wept. Not only were they losing many friends among the Hudson Bay men, but they knew that trade between the interior and the white men would no longer pass through Chinook hands.

Fort Vancouver was located on the north shore of the river, opposite where the Willamette River runs into the Columbia. When the Mountain Men who trapped for the Hudson Bay Company came into the post with their furs, they liked what they saw. When the time came to retire from the hard life of fur trapping, these men settled in the valley with their Indian wives and families. They were joined by trappers for American fur-trading companies, and so slowly a tiny community formed around Fort Vancouver and in the Willamette valley.

This small community of white men with Indian wives was no threat to the Indians of the northwest. But gradually word of the excellent farmland available on the Willamette spread east. A Methodist missionary to the men on the Willamette, Marcus Whitman, returned to the East singing the praises of the country.

It seems incredible that settlers would be willing to travel more than a thousand miles on foot, horseback, and by wagon, through deserts, across mountains, and often fighting hostile Indians, just to find better farmland. But this is what happened, and it happened almost overnight, as an "Oregon fever" seized the United States.

In 1841 the first small party of migrants arrived, more dead than alive. The next year a larger party arrived, having traveled for six months. The following year 800 men, women, and children reached Fort Vancouver, bringing with them several hundred head of cattle. This was more than twice the number of white settlers in the whole territory at the time. In 1844 the number doubled again, and in 1845 more than doubled again, until there were 6,000 settlers. Four years later the number was 9,000 and the flood kept coming, despite the hardships of the journey.

There were a number of reasons for the Oregon fever, aside from the stories of a "paradise" brought back to the East by Whitman and other missionaries. One was the promotion of western migration by politicians, who wanted to see the United States expand to the Pacific. And probably the most important fact was that many Americans who had settled in the Great Plains were fed up with cold winters. They wanted to make a new start.

The new settlers from the United States changed the far West, not only for the Indians, but also for the Hudson Bay trading post. The settlers arrived like an invasion. In a few years Oregon became American, not Canadian or British. And the Indians found themselves being crowded off their own lands.

The settlers wanted farmland, so they immediately cut down trees and cleared the land. The wild animals of the forests disappeared, and the Indians had no more hunting grounds. Also, the settlers treated the Indians in the area just as Americans treated Indians elsewhere—they took their lands and drove the Indians off by force if they objected.

The coastal lands did not make good farmland, so the whites were willing to leave those lands to the Indians. Although their wild game disappeared from the forests, they still had salmon, oolichan, and an occasional whale on the shore. The white man's diseases had reduced their numbers to a small fraction of what they had once been, so there was still enough food for all. And they did not die in battle—there were not enough of them left to fight if they had wanted to. They survived.

TOTEM POLES, "HOOTCH," AND GUNS

In the 1840s the lands to the south of Puget Sound were rapidly filling up with white settlers, but the land to the north remained untouched by the invasion. Nevertheless other causes led to drastic changes in the lives of the Indians there.

One cause of change was the loss of spirit in the population. When whole families, even whole villages were wiped out in a few days, the survivors naturally gave up. The Indians felt that they were a disappearing people to whom some great evil spirit of destruction had come. Many who lost their families and villages were ready to give up the ways of their ancestors. The old, Indian ways did not seem to make sense anymore.

The trade with European and American ships caused other changes. The Indians of the coast quickly adopted the white men's tools and materials to traditional Indian uses. Iron and steel tools were very popular with the Indians, but so were iron nails, which they learned to melt down and forge into tools themselves. The European's hatchet-head could be removed from its shaft and turned sideways to make an adze. Axes and saws made cutting down the tall cedar, fir, and spruce much easier. Steel chisels and hammers quickened the pace with which a canoe could be made, boards split from logs, or wood masks and house-posts carved.

Because the new tools and materials allowed the coastal Indians to do their traditional work more quickly and efficiently, the first effect of trade was to make the Indians even richer than before. The richer families had larger surpluses of everything. Meanwhile the poorer Indians, who had little or nothing to trade to the merchant ships, became poorer. Wealth became more important than ever among the coastal Indians.

Another effect of trading was that many Indian ways were abandoned and skills forgotten. Most of the Indians gave up everything to hunt sea otter. They became dependent upon the ships that visited them for things they had once made themselves. The white merchant ships brought blankets in great quantity, for instance, and they were cheap. It no longer seemed worthwhile to put many weeks of labor into weaving a blanket.

Iron pots and skillets also made life easier. But in many villages the result was that the Indians stopped making the ingenious, watertight baskets. Many simple, everyday tools, on which the Indians had lavished much attention and labor, were replaced by cheap, strong, steel tools.

The changes were not all bad. One of the most spectacular developments among the coast Indians in the nineteenth century was an increase in wood carving, especially of what has been called the "totem pole."

Totem poles had been made by some Indians before the arrival of steel tools. The Tlingit, for example, had traditionally used a single large log for the entrance-way to their lodges. Into this big log a doorway was carved. This house-post was usually no taller than the lodge itself and was carved to resemble an animal or supernatural beast, with the door as its mouth. Sometimes several other animals were also carved on the post, each one identified with the family living in the lodge. The animals represented branches of the family tree, or clans, and the animal that represented each clan was called a totem, or crest. These crests or totems

These are house posts showing Raven and family ancestor-spirits.

were carved on everything belonging to the family or clan. They were even woven into their blankets.

With the new steel tools the Indians' expert wood carvers found that they could carve much better and much faster. Their works became larger. The totem pole changed from a simple house-post carved with several crests to a tall, independent pole that reached 30 or 40 feet high and was covered over its entire length by crest-animals. Such a pole showed to everyone how proud its owners were of their ancestors.

Two other products of European civilization changed Indian life: guns and alcohol. The guns Baranov had complained about at New Archangel continued to be supplied by the sea merchants, especially the Americans. Eventually, when the Russians had enough supply ships of their own, American merchant ships were banned from Alaska for this reason. But the damage had been done, and the Russians did not have the navy to enforce the ban anyway. The guns were of little value to the

Model of house with totem pole. (Haida)

Indians for hunting. They were seldom accurate enough or trusty enough, and the noise they made drove away the game. But the guns were useful for fighting. They made the ambush style of fighting used by the coastal Indians much more deadly.

American trading ships also brought the Indians liquor. Some of the most important families among the coastal Indians tried to stop the Americans from trading liquor for furs and smoked salmon. They felt that the Indians lost dignity when they became drunk on white men's liquor. Even slaves laughed at a drunken Indian, no matter how many blankets he had in his lodge. But the white traders were glad to sell their liquor and did not care what it did.

Eventually the Indians learned to make alcohol themselves. Deserters from an American ship found a refuge among Tlingit Indians in a village called Hootchenu, and they repaid the Indians' hospitality by teaching them how to make alcohol from molasses. The Indians were soon making it in quantity, and it was called "hootchenu" after the village. Eventually the word was shortened to "hootch," a word still used in the United States for cheap or illegal liquor.

The new wealth brought to the Indians by the trading ships also changed one of the Indians' most important customs, the potlatch. As wealth increased and became more important, the potlatch became more prominent and much more wasteful. The situation was made worse by the reduction in the numbers of the Indians by disease. Often a wealthy family was completely wiped out by disease, or reduced to a few members. Then the question was, which family would take its place in ranking order? Families would hurry to throw giant potlatches to show how rich they were. Often, in the competition to seem rich and important, families spent far more than they could afford.

Among the Kwakiutl the potlatch reached its most extreme development. Indians borrowed, gambled, and even stole to throw bigger potlatches than their rivals. And the potlatches themselves were no longer the same. In order to exceed in extravagance all previous potlatches, some families accumulated their property in great heaps in front of their lodges—and burned it! By destroying their possessions they showed how rich they were. Blankets, canoes, cedar boxes full of valuables—all went into the big fire. The next family to have a potlatch had to burn even more possessions or lose face.

Although these potlatches were very destructive, and sometimes made beggars of once wealthy families, they remained important to the Kwakiutl and other Indians of the coast. They gathered everyone in the village together to share a feast. And in the rivalry, even in destruction, the Indians maintained a kind of order within the village.

While some Indians did not like the direction the potlatch was taking, they believed it was better than giving up their Indian ways altogether.

The Kwakiutl Indians—and the Tsimshian, Haida, Bella Coola, Nootka, and Salish—were now subject to the government of Canada in the province of British Columbia. The Canadian government disapproved of the destruction of property at the potlatches. Christian missionaries complained that the potlatch interfered with their efforts to make Christians of the Indians. So the Canadian government outlawed the potlatch, the winter ceremonies, and the spirit dances. In effect, they made it illegal for the Indian to follow Indian ways.

14

SAWMILLS, CANNERIES, AND GOLD

The first half of the 19th century was a period of rapid improvement in ocean navigation. Sailing ships were bigger and faster, steamships were invented and improved. As a result the Pacific coast of America was no longer as remote as it had once been. The nations of the world began to look for new ways to use the lands discovered by Cook, Vancouver, and Gray in other ways than trading for Indian furs.

In the brief period from 1840 to 1870 the map of the Pacific coast became much simpler. The Spanish had gradually lost or given up their claims to the Pacific coast, ending with the loss of Mexico.

In 1845 the young Mexican nation was defeated in a war with the United States and gave up her claim to upper California, although she kept the lower part, Baja California.

But both Great Britain and the United States claimed the land from northern California to Alaska. The British claimed it because of Cook's discoveries, and the establishment of the Hudson Bay posts of Fort George and Fort Vancouver. The United States claim was based on Gray's discovery of the Columbia River and the flood of Americans into the area after 1840. In 1848 an agreement was reached, giving the area of the present states of Oregon and Washington to the United States, and that of the Canadian province of British Columbia to Great Britain.

The Russian hold on Alaska remained weak. The fur hunting along the coast of Alaska grew worse, so the Russians tried the waters farther south. They established a post far down the coast of northern California, which they called Fort *Rossiya*— Russia—now Fort Ross. They hoped that they would find better hunting at this colony and also be able to grow food crops to keep New Archangel well supplied. The new colony did not work out, however. Eventually it was sold to an American, John Sutter—whose property near Sacramento, California, was the center of the famous gold rush of 1849.

Then in 1855, the Tlingit at Sitka once again staged an all-out attack on New Archangel. The Russian commander reported that if the Indians had cannon to blast down the fortress walls they would have succeeded in destroying the settlement. As a result the Russians decided to leave North America entirely, and in 1869 Alaska was sold to the United States for 7.2 million dollars. Most Americans at the time saw no point in owning what they thought was a frozen wasteland and called the purchase "Seward's Folly," or "Seward's Icebox," because Secretary of State William Seward had arranged it.

When the purchase was made, the Indians of Alaska were not even allowed inside the fortress to

Tlingit men at Sitka.

watch the changing of the flags. But they were soon aware that a change had taken place among the white men, which meant a change for them as well.

Although most Americans had no interest in Alaska, a few did, including settlers. In the first years after the purchase there was a rush of land-hungry settlers who hoped to get a new start in life. Most of these had no success. They found, as the Russians had before them, that there was little farming land. There was no way to live except by hunting, trapping, and fishing, as the Indians did, or by opening a shop in the village that had been New Archangel and was now Sitka.

The sea merchants were also interested in Alaska. American merchant ships had been banned in Alaska by the Russians for many years. But in the first year after the Alaska purchase, more than 70 American ships visited Sitka. Many went on to trade at Indian villages. The American merchants were aggressive and did not always treat the Indians fairly. And when the Indians fought them, the American government sent a naval ship to blast them out of existence.

The Americans did not control fur seal hunting as the Russians had. The Russians had learned from their experience with the sea otter not to overkill. Seals were killed by the thousands each year on a few small islands called the Pribilofs. After only a few years of American hunting, the seals were as rare as the almost extinct sea otter.

One of the most important changes for the Indians of Alaska was the arrival of new industries, especially sawmills and fish canneries. These affected the very basis of Indian life—cedar and salmon. Lumberjacks cut down the trees nearest the coast, as these were the easiest to bring to the mills. These were also just the trees needed by the Indians who had to float them to their villages. And *all* the trees in an area were cut, leaving none for the Indians and none to seed the ground for trees to grow in the future.

The canneries, which provided delicious salmon to the world, killed the fish in far greater numbers than the Indians did. The carefully balanced system in which villages or families owned the right to fish certain places only for certain periods of time was destroyed completely. The canneries got the first, the best, and soon almost *all* of the salmon.

The United States had no policy for Alaska or the people living there, and no interest in either. The territory was governed in turn by the U.S. Army, The U. S. Revenue Cutter Service, the U. S. Navy, and finally, after 1884, by a very weak territorial government. None of these governments showed any interest in protecting or helping the Indians. Indeed, the governments all viewed their job as chiefly one of protecting the new industries and the handful of non-Indian residents *from* the Indians.

The rapid disappearance of wood and salmon reduced the Indians to poverty. And no attempt was made to provide for those displaced by white settlers. The medical and educational needs of the Indians in this changing world were ignored. Alaska was America's "forgotten" province, and the Indians there were the forgotten people.

But the Indians learned to adapt to the changes. If they could no longer spear salmon from the river banks as they once had, then they must work for the canneries and accept wages for the work they did. Men caught the fish while the women, instead of weaving blankets and picking salmonberries, worked in the canneries, packing the fish in cans.

If the Indian could no longer cut down the tall cedar and float it to his village, he could go to work for the sawmills and cut down trees for wages. And it wasn't long before it was well known in Alaska that there was no better lumberjack than a Tlingit Indian.

Some Indians also found ways of turning their traditional arts into a way of making a living. In the 1880s steamboats began arriving in Alaska, bringing tourists from California and Oregon to see the famous "totem pole villages." These tourists provided an eager market for Indian handiwork, the

Tlingit handiwork, hand-woven baskets.

carved wood and bone, the hand-woven baskets and blankets. And as more tourists arrived, the fame of the Indians' art spread and the market for their work increased.

Working for wages also changed the way the Indians lived. Many villages were abandoned as the Indians left them to live near the sawmills and canning factories. It was no longer possible to share potlatches or winter dances with friends and relatives around the lodge fires. Even those Indians who lived by making blankets and carving had to move to where the tourists could conveniently reach them.

Perhaps the Alaskan Indians were lucky to be ignored. They fared better than most Indians in the United States, for American Indian policy usually aimed at destroying the Indians through war, or by taking away their lands, or reducing them to dependence on reservations. The Alaskan Indians worked out their own way of living with the changes brought by white men.

Raven had made the world, after all, and the traditions of the Indians of the Pacific coast told them that the world was full of sudden change and confusion. The Indians of Alaska learned to find a path from their old ways to the white men's ways without losing a sense of their Indian identity. When the white men opened schools they sent their children. They learned to read the white men's words as they had learned to use his tools. And it wasn't long before they learned to demand the rights that the white men's laws said they had.

15

REVIVAL

In 1881 a Squaxin Indian named John Slocum died. The Squaxin Indians were a small group of Salish-speaking Indians who lived on the shores of Puget Sound, in northwestern Washington. Years before, they had given up their lands. Now they were widely scattered and few in number.

Nevertheless, the death of the Squaxin John Slocum marked an important event in the history of all the Indians of the Pacific coast. Because John Slocum did not stay dead! In the middle of his funeral, with friends and relatives gathered around his sheet-draped body, Slocum unexpectedly sat up and began to speak.

Slocum was 40 years old. He was the father of 13 children, but many of these had died. He and his wife Mary lived on a tiny homestead near Olympia, Washington. Slocum, like many coast Indians, worked as a logger. He was poor, sometimes he drank too much. His head had been flattened as a child in the traditional Salish way, but the Slocums no longer believed in the traditional Indian customs. They had listened to white men's missionaries, but they had no religion.

But when John Slocum sat up and startled his friends and relatives, he spoke of religion. He said he had died and traveled to heaven. There he had spoken to angels of God. The angels told him he could not enter heaven because of his sinful life. He must return to earth and lead other sinful Indians to a Christian way of life.

Slocum said a church must be built, and the Indians built it. Then he began to preach, and he brought many Indians to Christianity. But after a while the excitement caused by his "death" and revival faded. Indians stopped coming to hear him preach. Slocum himself lost interest in Christianity and began to live as he had before.

Then he became ill a second time. A second time he approached death. His wife Mary suddenly began to shake and weep and moan at his bedside.

And to everyone's amazement, John Slocum began to recover. When he had fully recovered, he explained that his wife's uncontrollable shaking at his bedside had saved his life. The shaking was God's power taking hold of her body.

Thereafter, the "shaking" became part of the religion preached by the Slocums. Just as the spirits had once come to their Salish ancestors on winter nights, making them sing and dance, so now God's power came to the Shakers, as they were called. God's power made them shake and groan and weep. And when it was over the Shakers felt new strength to be good Christians.

The Shaker religion quickly spread to other Salish Indians of the Puget Sound area. Then it spread still farther, around the United States and Canada. It was a Christian religion, but it was also an Indian religion. John Slocum's journey to heaven to speak to angels was like a shaman's journey to the villages of spirits.

The Shaker religion appealed chiefly to just those Indians who had previously followed the way of life of the Northwest coast. It made it possible for these Indians to experience the white men's religion— but in their own way. It also gave them a religion they could practice in a world in which the village, the family lodge, the potlatch, and the winter ceremonies had all disappeared.

Farther up the coast, where towns and factories

were not so numerous, the Indians were able to hold onto more of their traditional life. Many Indians of British Columbia and Alaska tried to stay away from the white men's world as much as possible. They rejected the white men's religions and tried to keep to the old ways. But it wasn't easy.

Not only were the salmon taken by the canneries, the whales by the white whale hunters far out at sea, wild game chased away, and even the berry patches dug up for small farms, but the white men's laws often made life more difficult. In British Columbia the white Christian missionaries disapproved of the Indian religions. They called them "devil-worship." Didn't the masks they wore during the winter dances look like devils and monsters?

Other white men objected to the potlatch. It seemed criminal to them that the Indians, who were often very poor by white men's standards, destroyed large quantities of property for no purpose. They did not understand that the Indian village and the Indian way of life were held together by mutual gift-giving by families at potlatches. Nor did the white men have any right to interfere with what the Indians chose to do.

Although the potlatch and winter ceremonies were outlawed in Canada, many Indians continued to practice them in secret. They could not give up their traditional way of life without giving up their sense of who they were. They defied the white men's laws and refused the white men's religion.

Throughout the late 1800s and well into the 1900s the numbers of Indians on the Pacific coast continued to diminish. Those living their traditional life in Indian villages were even fewer. But gradually the downward trend stopped, and reversed itself. Indians of the Pacific coast are today becoming more numerous again, and they are also returning to their traditions.

In British Columbia in 1951 the government revoked the law making it illegal to practice the winter ceremonies or the potlatch. Indians no longer risked heavy fines or prison for practicing their own ceremonies.

The dances and songs are also still practiced by Salish and Salish-speaking Indians, such as the Nooksack, across the border in the United States. The Nooksack are a small group of Indians who never left their traditional homeland on Bellingham Bay near the Canadian border. The religion of the Nooksack is not exactly the same as in the old days, but it is similar. They still look for and find guardian spirits. There are song and dance "experts" who help the young. And the experience of being visited by spirits is expected to help the individual become a better man or woman. Many spirit dancers among the Nooksack are also Christians, some Shakers.

In Alaska, the Tlingit have taken the lead in bringing Indians and other native Americans into politics. The Alaskan Native Brotherhood— an organization of Aleuts, Eskimos, and Indians— has fought to protect Indian rights and to make sure that Indian views are heard by government.

One of the activities of the Brotherhood has been to encourage the education of Native Americans, and this campaign has been very successful. The Tlingit especially have taken to education. Many have become prominent in various professions and occupations in the state.

Many of the people of the Pacific coast have adapted completely to the world of the white men. Others live on reservations set aside for them, chiefly in Washington State around Puget Sound. But many other Indians have tried to find a life that connects the world of their Indian ancestors with the modern world.

Among the most successful of the Indians who live in both worlds are contemporary Indian artists. In recent years many Indians of the northwest coast have returned to the skills of their ancestors. They make blankets and baskets, sweaters and carvings, as their ancestors did a hundred years and more ago. Other Indian artists make new designs, especially in jewelry, designs that are nevertheless strongly inspired by the traditional ones.

And they find that the world beyond the Pacific coast of America is eager to buy the beautiful things they make.

So, although the traditional way has changed, it has not died out. Although disease destroyed many Indian villages, some remain. The number of Indians on the coast increases each year. As the numbers increase, the strength of their heritage grows stronger.

Where the high, snow-covered mountains fall steeply to the sea, and the thick mists blanket the narrow coves and inlets, a people still seeks guidance and inspiration from the spirits that spoke to its ancestors.

INDEX

A

adze, 31, 102
Alaska, 17, 38, 55, 68, 77, 78, 81, 94,
    105, 110, 111, 112, 113, 114, 116,
    120, 122
Alaskan Native Brotherhood, 122
Aleutian Islands, 77
Aleuts, 78–80, 81, 122
Americans, 75–76, 81, 84–89,
    96–100, 105, 106, 110
Antarctic Ocean, 63
Arctic Ocean, 68, 89
Astor, John Jacob, 88
Astoria, 88, 89, 90

B

Baja California, 110
Baranov, Alexander, 78–82, 105
Baranov Island, 78, 82
baskets (Indian), 22, 37 (picture),
    103, 115

Bear-men, 51
beaver furs, 89, 97
Bella Coola Indians, 19
Bellington Bay, Washington, 121
Bering, Vitus, 62, 77
Bering Sea, 62
Bering Strait, 77
Billings, Capt. Joseph, 78, 84, 85
blankets, 33 (picture) 103, 116
    -as money, 35–36
"Boston Men", 70, 72, 89
British, 63–69, 70–74, 77, 89–90,
    110
    See also English
British Columbia (Canada), 19, 38,
    108, 110, 120, 121

C

California, 16, 34, 55, 56, 57, 58, 61,
    62, 75, 110, 114
Canada, 89, 108, 110, 113, 120, 121

"candle fish." *See* oolichan
canneries, 113, 114, 115, 120
Cannibal Dancers. *See* Hamatsa
canoes, 30, 45, 64
Carlos IV, King of Spain, 70, 71, 74
cedar, 28–32, 113
chests (decorated), 46 (picture),
Chilkat robe (Tlingit), 33 (pictures)
China, 68, 69, 74, 96
Chinook Indians, 22, 86–88, 90,
    91–92, 93, 97, 98
"Chinook jargon" (language), 88
Chinook salmon, 24
clamons, 88
clans, 18
Clatsop Indians, 86–87, 93
Columbia River, 22, 75, 85–87, 89,
    93, 97, 98, 110
Cook, Capt. James, 63–69, 70, 77,
    78, 83, 84, 109, 110

D

dancing societies, 48–54
dentalium (shell), 35, 36 (picture)
Discovery, 64
Drake, Francis, 56–60, 61, 63, 64
Drake's Bay, 57

E

Elizabeth I, Queen of England, 56,
    57, 60
English, 56–60, 62.
    See also British
Eskimos, 122

F

flounder, 26
Fort Clatsop, 86, 87
Fort George, 90, 97, 110
Fort Ross, 110
Fort Vancouver, 97, 98, 99, 110
Fraser River, 25
Friendly Cove, 72, 74

G

George III, King of England, 71, 72,
    74, 90
Gitlakdamiy (Tsimshian village)
    picture, 17
"Golden Hind," 57
Gray, Capt. Robert, 75, 76, 88, 109,
    110
Great Britain, 75, 83, 88, 89, 110
guardian spirits, 41–48, 121
Gwayasclums (village), 29 (picture)

H

Haida Indians, 17, 18, 30, 32
    (picture), 34, 36 (picture), 38,
    81, 87 (picture), 93, 105
    (picture)
halibut, 26
haliotis (shells), 36 (picture)
Hamatsa, 49
hats (Indian), 31 (picture), 31–32
Hawaii, 63, 68
head flattening, 38, 66
herring, 26
herring rake, 26

hootchenu (liquor), 106
house posts, carved, 103–104
Hudson Bay Fur Company, 90, 97, 98, 99, 110, 112

I

influenza ("cold sick"), 91–93

J

Jefferson, Thomas, 84–85

K

kayaks, 78
Kelekum, 72–73
Kendrick, Capt. John, 75
Kwakiutl Indians, 19, 107, 108

L

labret, 39
languages (of Pacific Coast Indians), 16
Ledyard, John, 84–85
Lewis and Clark Expedition, 85–88, 89, 93
Louisiana Territory, 85

M

MacKenzie, Alexander, 89
Makah Indians, 20, 27
Makweena, 65, 67–68, 70–74, 76

Martinez, Esteben Jose, 71–74
masks (dance), 51–52, 120
     -pictures, 14, 22, 50, 52, 53, 79
Mexico, 58, 61, 109, 110
missions, Spanish, 62–63
Missouri River, 85
Miwok Indians, 57–60

N

"New Albion," 60, 63, 69
New Archangel, 80, 81, 82, 105, 110, 111, 112
New Zealand, 63
Noocksack Indians, 121
Nootka Indians, 20, 27, 30, 31 (picture), 35, 38, 39, 65–68, 67 (picture), 69, 70–75, 83, 86
Nootka Sound, 64, 71, 83
Nootka Treaty, 74–75
North West Fur Company, 89, 90
Northwest Passage, 56, 63, 68

O

Olympia, Washington, 118
Olympic Peninsula (Washington), 20, 27
oolichan (fish), 26, 100
Oregon, 38, 88, 95, 98, 110, 114

P

Pacific Fur Company, 88
Philippines, 61
Point Reyes National Park, 57

potlatch, 39–40, 106–108, 115, 119, 120, 121
Pribilof Islands, 112
promyshlenniki, 78
Puget Sound, 19, 20, 33, 38, 101, 117, 119, 122

Q

Quamichan (Salish village), 20 (picture)
Queen Charlotte Islands, 17, 93
Quileute Indians, 27
Quinaulte Indians, 27

R

Raven, 9–14, 41, 71
    -mask, 14 (picture), 22 (picture), 52 (picture), 104 (picture), 116
Resolution, 64
Russia, 88
Russians, 62, 77–82, 85, 94, 105, 110–111, 112

S

Sacramento, California, 110
Salish Indians, 19, 29, 117, 118, 119, 121
salmon, 23–26, 45, 59, 86, 100, 106, 113, 120
salmon caches, 25 (picture)
salmon weir, 24–26, 24 (picture), 45
San Diego Bay, 62
San Francisco Bay, 57, 63
sawmills, 113, 114, 115

scurvy, 64
sea lions, 26
sea otter, 26–27, 69, 75, 77, 90, 96, 102, 112, 113
seals, 26, 90, 112, 113
Seward, William, 111
Shaker religion, 117–119, 121
shamans, 47–48, 49 (picture), 92
Siberia, 62
Sitka (Alaska), 18 (picture), 78, 80, 111 (picture), 112
slavery, 37–38, 106
Slocum, John, 117–119
Slocum, Mary, 118
smelts, 26
"soul catchers," 49 (picture)
Spain, 75, 83, 88
Spanish, 57–58, 61–63, 65, 70, 109
spirit dancing, 45–46, 48–54, 108
Squaxin Indians, 117
sturgeon, 26
Sutter, John, 110
sweathouse, 94

T

Tlingit Indians, 17, 18, 30, 38, 39, 78–82, 94, 103, 106, 111, 114, 122
    -robes, 19 (picture)
    -blankets, 33, 36 (pictures)
    -hats, 42 (picture)
    -rattles, 43 (picture)
    -baskets, 115 (picture)
totem, 52 (picture), 103–104
    See also Guardian Spirit
totem poles, 103–104, 105 (picture), 114
"triangle trade", 75, 88, 97

Tsimshian Indians, 17, 18, 19
tsitsika, 50

U

United States, 75, 76, 83, 84, 85, 88,
    89, 99, 110, 111, 113, 119

V

Vancouver, George, 83, 84, 109
Vancouver Island, 20, 27, 35, 64, 84
Venyaminov, Bishop Ivan, 94

W

Wakash languages, 66
Washington (state), 19, 20, 38, 64,
    95, 110, 117, 122
weir. *See* salmon weir
whale hunting, 20, 27
whales, 20, 27–28, 100, 120
Whitman, Marcus, 98, 99
Willamette River, 89, 98
winter dances, 115, 119
    See also spirit dancing

Y

Yakutat Bay, 82